Studies of the New Testament and Its World

Edited by
JOHN BARCLAY
JOEL MARCUS
and
JOHN RICHES

RENEWAL THROUGH
SUFFERING

RENEWAL THROUGH SUFFERING

A Study of 2 Corinthians

A. E. Harvey

T&T CLARK
EDINBURGH

T&T CLARK LTD
59 GEORGE STREET
EDINBURGH EH2 2LQ
SCOTLAND

First published 1996

ISBN 0 567 08508 2

British Library Cataloguing-in-Publication Data
A catalogue record for this book is available
from the British Library

Page make-up by Trinity Typesetting, Edinburgh
Printed and bound in Great Britain by Bookcraft, Avon

Contents

Preface   ix

Abbreviations   xi

Chapter 1   The Tribulations in Ephesus   *2 Cor. 1.3–9*   1

Chapter 2   The Aftermath   *2 Cor. 1.10–4.6*   32

Chapter 3   The Renewing Experience   *2 Cor. 4.7–7.16*   55

Chapter 4   The Commissioning   *2 Cor. 8–9*   80

Chapter 5   The Apologia   *2 Cor. 10–13*   92

Chapter 6   Renewal through Suffering   112

Bibliography   130

Index of References   137

Index of Modern Authors   145

General Index   147

Preface

I have thought for many years that some of the profound but difficult language in chapters 4 and 5 of 2 Corinthians might best be explained by reference to the traumatic event alluded to in chapter 1. The opportunity to devote some serious research to this idea arose in a short period of study leave which I was able to spend at the Church Divinity School of the Pacific in 1991, and I am grateful to my hosts there for their warm hospitality and for free access to the splendid library facilities of the Graduate Theological Union. Discussion with colleagues in Oxford and London, for which I am also grateful, encouraged me to pursue the project, of which the main contours can be seen by reading the first and last chapters of this book. But to strengthen the thesis it seemed necessary to offer a complete reading of 2 Corinthians so as to reveal ways in which Paul's frequently obscure language may be illuminated by being set in the context of the experience he seems to have undergone not long before writing this letter. Chapters 2 to 5 offer such a reading, in as much detail as is required to make an acceptable case, but without any pretension to supply a full commentary on every verse. By this means I hope I may have succeeded in suggesting a legitimate approach to one of the most endlessly fascinating writings in the New Testament, an approach which may stimulate further research among scholars and, for a wider circle of readers, throw some light on the obscurer parts of the text.

Unless otherwise stated, extended quotations from the Bible are taken from *The Revised English Bible* (1989).

November 1995   A.E.H.

Abbreviations

AG	*A Greek-English Lexicon of the New Testament and other Early Christian Literature*, by W. F. Arndt and F. W. Gingrich (Cambridge and Chicago, 1957)
ANRW	*Aufstieg und Niedergang der römischen Welt* ed. H. Temporini and W. Haase (Berlin, 1972–)
AT	Author's translation
AV	Authorized Version
BEThL	*Bibliotheca ephemeridum theologicarum Lovanensium*
BGBE	*Beiträge zur Geschichte der biblischen Exegese*
BHT	*Bieträge zur historischen Theologie*
Bl-D	*A Greek Grammar of the New Testament and other Early Christian Literature* by F. Blass and A. Debrunner, E.T. and revision by R. Funk (Cambridge and Chicago, 1961)
BP	*Bibliotheca Patrum* (Oxford, 1845)
BWANT	*Beiträge zur Wissenschaft vom Alten und Neuen Testament*
CBQ	*Catholic Biblical Quarterly*
EKK	*Evangelisch-Katholischer Kommentar zum Neuen Testament*
E.T.	English Translation
EvTh	*Evangelische Theologie*
FRLANT	*Forschungen zur Religion und Literatur des Alten und Neuen Testaments*
FS	Festschrift
HJP	*A History of the Jewish People in the Age of Jesus Christ* by Emil Schürer, A New English Version revised and edited by G. Vermes and F. Miller (Edinburgh, 1973–87)
HNT	*Handbuch zum Neuen Testament*
HTR	*Harvard Theological Review*
ICC	*The International Critical Commentary*
j	Jerusalem Talmud
JB	Jerusalem Bible
JBL	*Journal of Biblical Literature*
JQR	*Jewish Quarterly Review*
JSNT	*Journal for the Study of the New Testament*

JSNTSS	*Journal for the Study of the New Testament, Supplement Series*
JTS	*Journal of Theological Studies*
KEK	*Meyers Kritisch-Exegetischer Kommentar über das Neue Testament*
LSJ	H. G. Liddell and Robert Scott, *A Greek-English Lexicon*, New Edition by H. S. Jones (Oxford, 1940)
LXX	Septuagint
M	Mishnah
MPG	J. P. Migne, *Patrologia Graeca*
N-A²⁷	E. Nestle and K. Aland, *Novum Testamentum Graece*, 27th edition (Stuttgart, 1993)
NovT	*Novum Testamentum*
NRSV	New Revised Standard Version
NTS	*New Testament Studies*
PGL	*A Patristic Greek Lexicon* ed. G. W. H. Lampe (Oxford, 1961–68)
PMG	*Poetae Melici Graeci* ed. D. L. Page (Oxford, 1962)
REB	Revised English Bible
RSV	Revised Standard Version
S-B	H. L. Strack and P. Billerbeck, *Kommentar zum Neuen Testament aus Talmud und Midrasch* (Munich, 1922–8)
SBLDS	*Society of Biblical Literature Dissertation Series*
SE	*Studia Evangelica*
SJT	*Scottish Journal of Theology*
SNTSMS	*Society for New Testament Studies Monograph Series*
SNTW	*Studies of the New Testament and Its World*, ed. John Barclay, Joel Marcus and John Riches
TDNT	*Theological Dictionary of the New Testament* ed. G. Kittel and G. Friedrich (E.T. Grand Rapids, 1964–76)
TWNT	*Theologisches Wörterbuch zum Neuen Testament* ed. G. Kittel and G. Friedrich (Stuttgart, 1957–1973)
Vg	Vulgate
VGT	J. H. Moulton and J. Milligan, *The Vocabulary of the Greek Testament, illustrated from Papyri and other non-literary sources* (London, 1930)
WUNT	*Wissenschaftliche Untersuchungen zum Neuen Testament*
ZNW	*Zeitschrift für die Neutestamentliche Wissenschaft*
ZThK	*Zeitschrift für Theologie und Kirche*

Chapter 1

The Tribulations in Ephesus

2 Corinthians 1.3–9

In this brief study of 2 Corinthians I shall argue that there was an event in the life of St Paul which fundamentally affected his understanding of the meaning of suffering, of his relationship with Christ, and of the help he could give to others when they found themselves in situations of comparable hardship. It is an event which has received surprisingly little attention from commentators and theologians; and yet I believe it holds the key to a number of the most complex and obscure passages in the letter. In other words, I shall maintain that in order to understand some aspects of Paul's theology we need first to attend to certain elements in his biography.

At first sight this may seem an unrealistic enterprise. There is no generally accepted 'biography' of Paul. Attempts to write one are notoriously unsatisfactory. The sources are tendentious and sometimes contradictory, the chronological sequence is at some points problematical, and the evidence fails us altogether at certain crucial points. Yet the amount of information we possess about Paul's life is quite impressive: we know a great deal less about Socrates or Confucius. Even for Jesus our information is almost all concentrated on the last two or three years of his life – we know virtually nothing about his upbringing, his education or his early friendships and interests, and we know of no event in his youth that might have had a formative influence on his later career. But for Paul we have the material for at least an outline biography. We know his place of birth (Tarsus, the capital of Cilicia); and this allows us to say something in general terms about his background and early upbringing. We know the name of one of his teachers (Gamaliel), from which we can infer the kind of education he received. Paul tells us himself about his interests, his enthusiasms and his attitude towards the first Christians with whom he came in contact.[1] Then came his conversion, described three times in Acts and alluded to (though in much less detail), in his own writings. From then on he was a traveller: we can plot his journeys on a map, and he tells us himself of some of the sensational vicissitudes he endured, including three shipwrecks and a number of public floggings. The story continues up to his final imprisonment in Rome; and we have credible information from later sources that, possibly after a further voyage to Spain, he was martyred under the Emperor Nero in the mid-sixties CE.[2]

Not all of this is equally reliable. When Paul writes about himself, we sometimes have to allow for some rhetorical exaggeration or self-deprecation. The information that comes from Acts does not always square with Paul's own testimony; when it tells us something that Paul does not mention we cannot be sure we can trust it.[3] But the outline is clear and beyond any reasonable doubt. It includes events dramatic and unexpected enough to affect the thinking of anyone who had to undergo them. Modern biographers instinctively look for moments in their subjects' lives that were crucial for their development. Any life of Paul would include several incidents of this kind. We would expect to find that his attitude to many things was affected by what he experienced. Can we trace such changes through his letters?

This is a question which does not seem often to have interested Paul's interpreters.[4] For one thing, his surviving letters span little more than a decade. The only really formative event in his life – his conversion – took place at least fifteen years before he wrote any of them. Should we really expect to find radical changes in his thinking in a period when he was primarily engaged in building on and consolidating his great missionary achievements of earlier years?

---

[1] The evidence for Paul's early life is assembled and discussed by M. Hengel, *The Pre-Christian Paul* (E.T. London and Philadelphia, 1991).

[2] For a convenient, if conservative, discussion of the evidence for Paul's last years and death, see F. F. Bruce, *Paul: Apostle of the Free Spirit* (Exeter, 1977) chapter 37.

[3] See below, chapter 5. n. 1.

[4] An exception is B. M. Ahern, 'The Fellowship of his sufferings (Phil. 3.10)' *CBQ* 22 (1960) 1–32, who writes, 'During the first months at Corinth he went through a maturing process which vitally developed his thought' (p. 1). However he gives no attention to 2 Cor. 1.8.

Moreover, Paul's letters are part of Scripture; that is to say, any part of them can be and has been appealed to for guidance in the Christian faith without regard to the stage in his life at which it was written. If there appears to be some difference of emphasis or meaning between one passage and another, this has more often been regarded as a problem to be solved by technical hermeneutical methods than as an opportunity to trace a development of thought:[5] it has seemed more important to show that Paul taught a consistent Christian doctrine, and so to 'reconcile' or 'harmonize' apparent contradictions, than to explore any possible changes that Paul's thinking may have undergone. The fact that a body of writings is regarded as Scripture tends to make it appear flat and undifferentiated: any sentence is as authoritative as any other, and there is no point in asking when and why it was written.

Recently, it is true, this reverent assumption that every word written by Paul is of timeless importance has given way to a more critical approach. Emphasis is now laid on the fact that Paul's writings are *letters*[6] – real letters, for the most part, each sent on a particular occasion to address a particular set of issues and each written in the tone and the style most likely to create the desired response in the recipients. To quote a phrase from an American scholar, each is 'a word on target in the midst of human, contingent specificity'.[7] It follows that to understand Paul's thinking we have to try to reconstruct every aspect of the situation to which each letter was addressed. We have to recognize that he was bound to say things differently according to changing circumstances – according to a different 'target' – even if his fundamental message was the same. We cannot hope to understand Paul unless we can understand also the specific circumstances which caused him to write as he did.

---

[5] Though Origen claimed he could trace Paul's spiritual development from 1 Corinthians to Romans, *Comm. in Rom.* Praef. (*MPG* 14. 834). To the objection that there was not much time for such development between one epistle and the next, Origen boldly replied that if the space of time between 1 and 2 Corinthians was sufficient for the sinner convicted of incest to repent and be received back into the church, surely the apostle with his more rapid rate of progress would have made a significant advance during the same period!

[6] See J. L. Bailey and L. Vander Broek, *Literary Forms in the New Testament* (London, 1992) 23–31.

[7] J. C. Beker, *Paul the Apostle* (Philadelphia, 1980) 24.

Even so, the focus of attention does not seem to have been upon Paul himself. There has been intense interest in the circumstances of the churches to which he wrote, the pressures they were under, the changes which may have occurred in their Christian perceptions. But the possibility that equally important changes may have taken place in the writer himself has seldom been allowed for. The sometimes traumatic experiences he underwent make no appearance in any analysis of his thought. As a tool for reconstructing his theology, the remarkably detailed biographical materials that are available are quietly left on the shelf.

To all this there is of course one great exception: the conversion. No one doubts that Paul's encounter on the Damascus road had a profound effect on him; indeed his letters, though some of them were written at least two decades later, may be described as still working out the consequences of that momentous experience. Not that it has always been seen as a key to understanding them: for many centuries the important thing about the conversion was what Paul (or whoever wrote the Pastorals) said about it himself: 'Because I acted in the ignorance of unbelief I was dealt with mercifully' (1 Tim. 1.13). It was something that could be held up as a supreme example of the loving forgiveness of God – if he forgave even the zealous persecutor of the church, how much more will he forgive you and me, who are Christians![8] But any Christian who has a powerful conversion experience himself may feel some resonance with that experience when he reads the story of the Damascus road or Paul's own account of having been 'killed' by sin (Rom. 7.13) in his early life, and assume that Paul's conversion had the same cause and the same dynamics as his own. The most notable and influential instance of this was the 'conversion' of Martin Luther from what he came to regard as an excessive preoccupation with 'works of the law' in the Roman Catholic church of his time to the perception of the free grace of God imparted to, but never earned by, the penitent sinner. It seemed to Luther that Paul's attempt to gain merit from God through the observance of the complex rules of behaviour demanded by his Pharisaic ideals had led

---

[8]   E.g. Chrys. *Hom. 3 in 1 Tim.* (BP pp. 22–30).

to a conversion experience similar to his own[9] – an interpretation which has dominated, not only the study of Paul, but the greater part of Reformation theology for the last four hundred years.[10]

In the nineteenth century a further impetus was given to the study of Paul's conversion by Freudian psychology. The conversion is of course described in the New Testament as totally sudden and unprepared, a miraculous intervention which caused Paul to make a radical change in his beliefs, his outlook and his activities. But, after Freud, everyone claimed to know that this is not how such things happen. The Damascus Road experience was seen as a classic instance of the release of forces that had been building up in the unconscious long before.[11] Paul's unsuccessful attempts to fulfil the most exacting demands of the Jewish law had gradually accumulated a load of subconscious guilt such that only the recognition of the impossibility of the task and the sudden insight into another way of pleasing God could provide any relief. The 'conversion' was in fact the discharge of long pent-up energies and frustrations in a way that created an overwhelming sense of liberation and new purpose. Similar experiences are induced again and again by psycho-analysis.[12] In the light of them, much that Paul says about himself seems to fall into place. For many, his conversion has become a paradigm of release from that sense of guilt which is one of the afflictions of modern western society.

In recent years all these reconstructions have come under severe criticism. If the conversion is seen primarily in moral terms – as a moment at which someone comes to see his or her entire way of life as inherently sinful and is led to a fundamental change of outlook – it can be asked, where does Paul use such negative language about his early life? Does he not actually show pride in his achievements and qualifications, seeing them, not as something sinful, but as advantages

---

[9] See his Preface to the Epistle to the Romans, final (or penultimate in editions after 1539) paragraph.

[10] A notable reaction to this is in Krister Stendahl, *Paul among Jews and Gentiles* (London, 1977). Cf. especially 16–17.

[11] For a typical example, see W. L. Knox, *Paul* (London, 1932) 36–7: 'In the depths of his soul a conflict was raging, ready to burst with the greater violence the more sternly it was repressed' etc.

[12] Cf. the classic account of such experiences by William Sargant, *Battle for the Mind* (London, 1957).

to be gladly surrendered for the sake of the new status of one forgiven and accepted through Christ? Those passages in Romans 7 which so tellingly describe the moral struggles that take place deep in the heart must not be arbitrarily assumed to refer only to Paul's pre-conversion experience,[13] as if they were descriptions of a tension which belonged only to his early life; they describe the realities of moral effort even for the mature Christian, as the writings of countless saints will testify. If his conversion is seen primarily as the moment when he abandoned the hopeless effort to fulfil detailed observances in favour of a life lived entirely in the free unmerited grace of God, why does he describe himself as having been 'irreproachable' in respect of righteousness according to the law (Phil. 3.6)? Is there evidence of any pious Pharisee of his time finding these observances impossible to fulfil? And if the psychological approach is adopted, according to which the 'conversion' was simply the inevitable explosion set off by a long accumulation of feelings of guilt and inadequacy, why does neither Paul nor the author of Acts give any hint of it and where, in any case, is the evidence that *guilt* for the past was any part of Paul's makeup?[14]

None of this is to deny that Paul's conversion was a profound experience which influenced every aspect of his thinking; it is merely a warning against using any one interpretation of that experience as a key to understanding his letters. And in any case we have to allow a period of at least fifteen years between the conversion and the first of Paul's surviving letters: whatever changes it produced in his thinking must have settled down into firm convictions well before he wrote any of them. What we are in search of are signs of changes which took place in his thinking between one letter and another and of events in his life which might have caused these changes. But here we are faced with another difficulty. We can trace change or development in Paul's letters only if we can be sure what order they were written in. But in many cases this is quite uncertain. 1 Thessalonians can be confidently regarded as the first surviving letter,[15] Romans as one of the last; but

---

[13] For an extended account and discussion of the options in the interpretation of Romans 7, see J. A. T. Robinson, *Wrestling with Romans* (London, 1979) 82–91.

[14] See, for example, E. P. Sanders, *Paul and Palestinian Judaism* (London, 1977) 409.

[15] Though it is possible, on the 'South Galatian' hypothesis, to date Galatians before 1 Thessalonians.

where Galatians comes, for example, depends on a number of historical factors about which scholars continue to disagree. And in any case the time-span covered by the letters is relatively short – fifteen years at most. Even if we knew exactly what order they were written in, could we expect to be able to chart any significant developments in the course of them?

But we must not exaggerate: certain landmarks can be identified despite the general chronological fog. If 1 Thessalonians is the first extant letter, and if in a later letter Paul seems to modify or contradict what he said there, it is at least possible that some event in his life had caused a change in his views or attitudes. It was one of the most influential of British post-war scholars, C. H. Dodd, who most notably found some mileage in this suggestion.[16] He drew attention to two matters on which Paul seems to have taken a particularly rigid line in 1 Thessalonians but about which he became more moderate later on; and his explanation was, for once, biographical: it was the influence of certain circumstances and experiences which caused Paul to change his mind and re-write his theology.

The first of these matters was Paul's attitude to the Jewish people. In 1 Thessalonians, as a result of their opposition to the Christian mission and their persecution of the newly-founded church, Paul consigns them to utter perdition: 'The wrath of God has come upon them with complete finality' (εἰς τέλος, 1 Thess. 2.16). In Romans, however, he can ask whether they have really fallen or merely stumbled, and can answer that it was indeed only a stumbling, a stumbling that has led to the salvation of others and will one day lead even to the restoration of Israel to its rightful place in the purposes of God (Rom. 11.11). Clearly these two passages cannot be reconciled, and Dodd took what in the history of Pauline studies must be judged an unusual step. He assumed a biographical reason. It was as a result, perhaps, of mature reflection, or possibly of some more positive encounters with Jewish enquirers, that Paul revised his theology.

The second matter is to do with Paul's personal hopes and expectations. In 1 Thessalonians, and again in 1 Corinthians, Paul

[16] 'The Mind of Paul', first published in 1934, reprinted in *New Testament Studies* (Manchester, 1953) 108ff.

clearly stated that he expected to be alive when Christ returned in glory. By the time he wrote 2 Corinthians and Philippians he was evidently not so sure. Now clearly this expectation was vulnerable to the vicissitudes of life. If Paul ever knew himself to be in serious danger of sudden death he must have been aware he could have no certainty about being still alive on the glorious day. But it must also be put in the context of what most Christians had been taught to believe in the early days of the church. For a while, at least, they expected the second coming to take place within the lifetime of their own generation. But in due course this somewhat naive belief must have yielded to a more mature realization that history was likely to have more time to run and that they could not count on any dramatic change taking place before they died. Paul would have been no exception to this; and C. H. Dodd used this biographical factor to explain the apparent shift of his position over the question whether he would personally be alive to see Christ's return. It has to be said that the evidence does not really support his view that Paul, along with others, was beginning to abandon the expectation of Christ's imminent return.[17] So far as we can tell from his letters, Paul never did abandon his belief that Christ would return in glory within a relatively small number of years. His generation was certainly that of which it could be said that 'on us the end of the ages has come' (1 Cor. 10.11). What is at stake is the more specific question whether, towards the end of his life, Paul still expected to be alive himself when this took place. It is here that we can reasonably ask whether there was some event in Paul's life which caused him to feel less confident. In C. H. Dodd's words, 'It seems probable that the extreme danger of death in which he had recently stood helped him to alter his outlook in this respect.'[18] For Paul does in fact describe such an incident:

We despaired even of remaining alive. (2 Cor. 1.8 AT)

Whatever it was that happened – and we shall see that there are difficulties in reconstructing it precisely – it was clearly not the

[17] Dodd is hard put to it, for example, to explain how Romans 13.11–14 represents a less urgent view of the imminent End than does the language of 1 Thessalonians.
[18] Op. cit. 111.

sort of event one would expect a biographer to pass over in silence, particularly as (for once) it is datable: it took place between the writing of 1 and 2 Corinthians. And, as we shall see, its social and religious implications must have been profound. Yet it has received strangely little attention from either point of view. Biographers seem to have missed its significance for understanding the development of Paul's self-understanding; theologians have missed its implications as a serious break in the continuity of Paul's thinking; and New Testament scholars have failed to recognize it as a key to much of the dense and impassioned argumentation of 2 Corinthians.

We must now subject this incident to closer investigation.

> We do not want you to be ignorant, my brothers, of the tribulations we endured in Asia, how we were excessively afflicted, yes even beyond our powers of resistance, so that we despaired of remaining alive. (2 Cor. 1.8 AT)

What had happened?

To the modern reader, these words look like an introduction to a full account of the episode. Paul wants the Corinthians to know about it, and we expect him to go on and tell them. To our surprise, he says virtually nothing more about it. Was it illness? Accident? Persecution? He leaves us guessing; and ever since patristic times[19] his interpreters have been divided on the matter. Even modern advances in our knowledge of the 'common' Greek used by Paul have not settled the question. Certainly the word Paul uses for 'afflicted' (ἐβαρήθημεν) occurs many times in connection with illness in letters on papyrus that have been discovered in Egypt in the last hundred years.[20] But this does not greatly help us, for it was a common word which could just as well be used, for example, in connection with taxation[21] – indeed Paul himself uses it elsewhere of laying a financial burden on others and so 'afflicting' them.[22] Moreover the other word Paul uses here –

---

[19] Cf. the account of different interpretations of the 'thorn in the flesh' (2 Cor. 12.7) given by J. B. Lightfoot, *Galatians* (London, 1905) 186–91.

[20] Instances in Windisch 45 n. 4.

[21] VGT s.v. βαρεῖν.

[22] In the form ἐπιβαρεῖν 2.5: 1 Thess. 2.9; 2 Thess. 3.8.

'tribulation', θλῖψις – is a regular term for persecution. There is nothing in either the passage or its context which will definitely settle the question.

But perhaps Paul tells us more about it elsewhere. Does he not refer in other places to something equally serious? Later in the same letter he gives a list of tribulations, any one of which might have called into question his powers of survival. And in his letter to the Christians in Galatia he tells us that his preaching there had been bedevilled by some extremely embarrassing 'weakness of the flesh', in response to which they would have 'given their eyes' to help him (Gal. 4.13–15). There is also the famous 'thorn in the flesh' (2 Cor. 12.7) that Paul likens to an 'angel of Satan' and that clearly impeded his work and shattered his self-esteem. It is possible to put all this together and reconstruct a medical history centred on some chronic complaint of the eyes[23] and liable to erupt into a crisis such as could nearly have cost Paul his life shortly before he wrote 2 Corinthians. A diagnosis along these lines has often been attempted. An eye condition, epilepsy,[24] headaches,[25] and many other recurrent conditions have been suggested.[26] But all these suggestions fail, not only because Paul does not tell us enough about his symptoms, but because we can never be sure how literally he intends us to take him. How are we to know that the words he used to the Galatians – 'giving their eyes to help him' – were not a figurative turn of phrase, exactly as they would be today?[27] How can we be sure that the 'thorn in the flesh' was a physical ailment at all? In the Greek Bible the word σκόλοψ was regularly used metaphorically (as it is today) for personal enemies;[28] and Paul's words could well be taken to mean (as they were by some of the Greek

---

[23] Dr J. Brown, cited by Lightfoot, *Galatians* 191 n. 1.

[24] Suggested by Albert Schweitzer, *The Mysticism of Paul the Apostle* (E.T. London, 1931) 153; M. Dibelius and W. Kümmel, *Paulus* (Berlin, 1956) 39.

[25] Tertullian, Jerome, Pelagius and others. Cf. Lightfoot *Galatians* 186.

[26] H. Clavier, 'La Santé de l'Apôtre Paul', *Studia Paulina* (FS de Zwaan, Haarlem, 1953) 66 n. 1 lists 37 suggested maladies. Cf. also U. Heckel, Der Dorn im Fleisch, Die Krankheit des Paulus in 2 Kor 12, 7 und Gal 4, 13f.' *ZNW* 84 (1993) 65–92, 80.

[27] Horace, *Sat.* 2.5.35; cf. M.-J. Lagrange, *Epître aux Galates* (Paris, 1942) 114. It is true, however, that the metaphor is not otherwise attested in Greek, and the Latin parallels are not exact.

[28] Num. 33.55; Ezek. 28.24 LXX.

Fathers,[29] who knew the language better than we do) some form of persecution, an 'angel of Satan' assuming the guise of a particularly persistent and ruthless opponent. In short, we get no further towards defining the 'tribulations we endured in Asia' by bringing in the witness of other passages. All Paul's references to his personal sufferings are expressed with the same tantalizing vagueness.

Yet this very failure of the text to provide the answer we are looking for may be significant: we may be asking the wrong question. Indeed, it is precisely in this area of illness, misfortune and adversity that our modern interests and assumptions have become strikingly different from those of the ancient world. Faced with evidence of sickness, our instinct is to ask what physical or psychological cause can be assigned to these particular symptoms; and so the main thrust of our questions will be towards an accurate description of the symptoms themselves. In Paul's time the question was different: not, What is wrong with me? but, Who has done this to me? Myself? Someone else? A demon? God? For this purpose an exact description of the symptoms or the misfortune was not particularly relevant; more important was the question what the sufferer felt like – guilty or angry, hopeful or despairing – and what the prospects were for restoring morale and self-respect.[30] Medical anthropologists make a distinction between disease and illness.[31] 'Disease' is simply a malfunctioning of the body: much of modern medical science is devoted to identifying it and curing it without reference to any particular personal factors or social circumstances. I take my migraine or my allergy to the doctor and he prescribes a cure appropriate to *that* disease in the hope that it will be appropriate also to me. 'Illness' is a much wider term. It embraces my response, and that of my social environment,[32] to a disease. It is what

---

[29] At least as early as Chrysostom, though on dogmatic, not linguistic, grounds. For references, see Lightfoot *op. cit.* 187. Cf. T. Y. Mullins, 'Paul's Thorn in the Flesh', *JBL* 76 (1957) 299–303. U. Heckel, art. cit. 76–7 argues that the patristic interpretation (starting with Tertullian *Pud.* 13. 15–16) of the affliction as an illness is more reliable than that which suggests persecution.

[30] K. Seybold and U. Mueller, *Sickness and Healing* (USA: Abingdon Press, 1978–81) 44–5.

[31] A. Kleinman, *Patients and healers in the context of culture* (Univ. of California Press, 1980) 72ff.

[32] Seybold and Mueller, 45–6.

gives physical symptoms a meaning; it is a construct which enables the sufferer to come to terms with a diseased condition and find some meaning in it. Defining the illness is a matter not just for doctors but for friends, social workers and priests. Paradoxically it can even be the first step to a cure, in that it places a strange and threatening sensation of disease in a framework of acceptance and hope.

There have of course always been those who have a morbid preoccupation with their symptoms[33] and who will talk about their problems mainly in terms of disease. But in the ancient world it was far more common to talk about illness, and in the Bible it is very rare indeed to hear about symptoms: it is rather the total situation of the sufferer, his relationship with God and his fellow-citizens, that occupies the centre of attention. This can be illustrated again and again from those of the psalms that are clearly expressions of personal suffering. One of the recurring themes in these psalms is that of the righteous sufferer, convinced of his own innocence, and struggling to understand how a just God can allow him to be brought almost to 'despair of life itself'. Yet, as in the case of Paul, the details of the affliction are left tantalizingly vague. Occasionally precise symptoms seem to be described:

> My strength drains away like water
> and all my bones are racked ...
> My mouth is dry as a potsherd
> and my tongue sticks to my gums. (Ps. 22.14–15)

A doctor might say that, despite the poetic language, these are familiar symptoms sufficient for a preliminary diagnosis: the psalmist is clearly ill. But immediately before this come the words:

> A herd of bulls surrounds me,
> great bulls of Bashan beset me.
> Ravening and roaring lions
> open their mouths wide against me. (vv. 12–13)

---

[33] Such as the notable literary invalid Aelius Aristeides.

So is it all metaphorical after all? Is the real problem, not a physical illness (though this may be present too), but the taunts and the heartless indifference of the ungodly? Is it a case of the adversity a man may bring on himself in this wicked world by refusing to compromise his moral and religious principles? As in the case of St Paul, modern interpreters are divided;[34] but clearly our question is not one that was of primary interest to the psalmist. What mattered to him, and to anyone in his situation at that time, was not the medical history of the sufferer but the social and religious predicament in which his suffering placed him. The question, that is, was not that of the diagnostician of today, who will ask, 'Where does it hurt most?' – but rather that of the sympathetic counsellor or (from a different point of view) of the complacent rival anxious to take advantage of the situation, 'What have you done that has brought you to this?'

This preference for speaking of illness rather than disease may help us to understand why Paul seems so reluctant to describe the nature of the personal crisis he has just been through, even though he appears to have promised to do so: our questions are not the ones that a man of his time and culture would normally think of answering. But there is another factor. There is, as we have said, a considerable amount of autobiographical material in Paul's letters; and 2 Corinthians provides some striking examples. But we must be careful not to read any of these recitals as if they were simply a matter of Paul keeping his correspondents up to date in his own doings. A modern letter writer may find it natural to include in a letter to a friend a chronicle of events in which he has been involved personally, particularly if these have caused inconvenience or suffering. But Paul's letters are seldom, if ever, to be thought of in such simple and personal terms. They were not written just to pass on interesting information about himself. Any references to his achievements or his vicissitudes had more serious motives – to prove a point, to mount a defence, to disarm criticism. As such, they ceased to be unselfconscious narratives of personal

---

[34] A. Weiser, *The Psalms* (London, 1962) 220. K. Seybold, *Das Gebet des Kranken im Alten Testament* (BWANT 99, Kohlhammer: Stuttgart etc., 1973) 76 allows only two psalms (of which Ps. 22 is not one) to be genuinely inspired by personal illness.

interest; they became examples of well-known techniques of persuasion.[35] In short, we cannot expect Paul to tell us exactly what happened to him on a given occasion as if it were a matter of neutral and objective information. We have to ask what led him to such personal matters in the first place and with what intention he dwells on them. What were the conventions governing the use of personal experiences to reinforce an argument? Would the writer have achieved his purpose better by a touch of exaggeration or by ironic self-deprecation? Teachers of rhetoric gave much attention to such questions. Paul's letters are certainly not rhetorical exercises; but nor are they merely personal bulletins on the writer's health and doings. They are serious attempts to persuade; and as such they can be expected to have observed at least the ground-rules of rhetorical practice with regard to such delicate matters as the defence of strongly-held principles, the rebuttal of accusations regarding personal conduct and the manner in which a person who claimed to live by philosophical or religious principles faced up to misfortune, failure or calumny. This is not to say, of course, that Paul deliberately made use of rhetorical techniques to strengthen his case. On more than one occasion he vigorously repudiates any such intention. But his readers, in Corinth and elsewhere, lived in an environment where public speaking and the arts of persuasion had a ready public and were highly esteemed.[36] At the very least, Paul will have needed to be sensitive to the reactions which such people were likely to have to anything which savoured of boasting or self-commendation. In any form of public communication autobiographical information could never be neutral: it could have the desired effect only if it were presented in such a way as to disarm criticism and avoid giving offence.

That Paul is making a point by recalling his past experiences, and not merely reminiscing for the interest of his readers, is evident beyond any doubt in the autobiographical passage in Galatians 1, where he describes the events which immediately followed his conversion for

---

[35] See George Lyons, *Pauline Autobiography: Toward a new Understanding,* SBLDS 73 (Atlanta, GA, 1985); J. Bailey and L. Vander Broek, *Literary Forms* 31–37.

[36] See the excellent discussion of this in Duane Litfin, *St Paul's Theology of Proclamation, SNTSMS* 79 (Cambridge, 1994) 124–6.

the purpose of establishing his claim to an authority independent of that of the Jerusalem apostles. But there are also passages in 2 Corinthians in which Paul gives a good deal of information about his recent experiences, and which we might be tempted to regard as more or less neutral and factual accounts. But here again there are other factors to be taken into account. What Paul gives us are lists of the trials and vicissitudes he has endured, sometimes of a quite sensational nature. There is no need to doubt the essential veracity of these accounts: Paul was certainly not making them up. But we still have to ask what his purpose was, and whether it would have been in his interest either to minimize or to exaggerate what he had been through. Consider the most specific and detailed of these recitals (2 Cor. 11), which begins with public floggings and shipwrecks, and works through various kinds of hazards and privations until it ends with his dramatic escape from Damascus in a basket let down from the wall. The passage begins with a direct comparison between Paul and his critics: he has to show that he is in no respect inferior to them. But this places it immediately in the literary category of 'comparison' (σύγκρισις), one of the standard means by which an orator would strengthen his case:[37] if he could show himself in every respect superior to his opponents, their charges against him would lose credibility. A few verses later, Paul uses a tell-tale phrase, 'If I must boast ...'. The question of how far a recital of one's own achievements would advance one's case was much discussed by rhetoricians:[38] to say too much about them might sound like 'boasting' and be counterproductive; to say too little might appear like an equally damaging false modesty. And even this is not all. The list of vicissitudes, however true to Paul's personal experience, is nevertheless typical of a well-known philosophical gambit. The Stoic philosopher – and still more the Cynic – prided himself on his indifference to physical and mental suffering, and would often give a recital of what he had been through in order to demonstrate the power of philosophy to make one able to rise above

---

[37] Cf. C. Forbes, 'Paul's Boasting and the Conventions of Hellenistic Rhetoric', *NTS* 32 (1986) 1–30.

[38] Plutarch devoted a whole treatise to the subject: *De laude ipsius (Mor.* 539A–547F). See J. T. Fitzgerald, *Cracks in an Earthen Vessel: An Examination of the Catalogues of Hardships in the Corinthian Correspondence,* SBLDS 99 (Atlanta, GA, 1988) 107–116.

such purely external and short-term vicissitudes.[39] We shall see later on that Paul's own account differs from these philosophical examples in important respects: he does not play down the degree of suffering involved in the way that Stoic philosophy demanded. There is also an element of his Jewish background to be taken into account. Those whose religious beliefs led them to take seriously the prospect of an imminent new age to be inaugurated by God – and Paul was certainly one of these – tended to regard any sequence of tribulations as a significant prelude to the great reversal which they awaited. We would do Paul an injustice if we were to read his account as no more than an exercise in any one of these *genres*; but we shall misunderstand him if we do not allow for him having been influenced by them, or at least having been aware of the risks involved in appealing to his own personal experiences. Given the conventions governing any such autobiographical references, we must not assume that what he tells us is to be taken without at least a pinch of salt.

It is therefore all the more significant that none of these stylistic or conventional considerations seem to apply to the passage with which we are concerned.[40] In the opening paragraph of 2 Corinthians, Paul does not appear to be on the defensive; he is not comparing himself with others; he is not assembling a series of experiences for the purpose of showing his endurance, his independence or his superiority. The immediate context is a prayer of thanksgiving – 'Blessed be the God and father of our Lord Jesus Christ ...' (1.3) – which introduces two themes that are of great importance in the letter. One is that of 'consolation' (παράκλησις), a word which defies translation into English.[41] It has survived into modern Greek in the form of a very common expression: παρακαλῶ – 'please'. But even this preserves an essential strand of the word's original meaning, that of any kind of urgent appeal. If I need your help, I can urge you to give it: I 'appeal'

---

[39] Fitzgerald, *op. cit.* ch. 3, especially p. 49.

[40] It is of course possible to see even 1.8 as a rhetorical ploy to enlist the sympathy of the audience/readers. See F. W. Hughes, 'The Rhetoric of Reconciliation: 2 Cor. 1.1–2.13 and 7.5–8.24' in D. F. Watson, ed. *Persuasive Artistry* (*JSNTSS* 50, 1991) 246–61 at p. 251: 'Paul perhaps exaggerates in 1.8–10 how terrible his sufferings were.' But he appears not to allow for the context of prayer and thanksgiving.

[41] Barrett, 60; cf. Martin, 9; O. Schmitz, *TWNT* 5. 792–8.

to you. If I find you downcast I can speak to you insistently in order to save you from despair: I 'console' you or 'comfort' you. If I find you doing wrong, I can remonstrate with you: I 'abjure' you. If you are offended, I can 'apologize' to you. All these usages stem from the fundamental sense of urgent address present in the verb παρακαλῶ, and can be traced also in its derivative 'paraclete': the one who can be appealed to to give help on the day of judgement, who can give consolation ('comfort') and moral guidance ('he will lead you into all truth'). Here, the primary sense is that of comfort or consolation: it is God who 'consoles us in all our tribulation so that we can console those who are in any kind of tribulation with the consolation by which we are consoled by God' (1.4). Yet the inadequacy of this translation becomes apparent when Paul goes on to his second theme, namely that this power to 'console' is a direct consequence of his own share in the sufferings of Christ: his own experiences do not merely enable him to show a kind of consoling sympathy with the sufferings of others, but provide him with a positive interpretation of suffering that he must now communicate with urgency and loving concern. The 'consolation' of his παράκλησις merges into vigorous encouragement and exhortation.

The word is not a new one in Paul's writings, but there is something arresting about the stress he places upon it here: the word occurs, either as a verb or a noun, no fewer than ten times in as many lines of Greek. Quite new also is the connection he makes between this consolation/encouragement and the experience of suffering, which he already begins to interpret as some kind of sharing in the sufferings of Christ. None of this is obvious or conventional. As so often, Paul has used a familiar form of expression – in this case, a prayer of blessing such as occurs again and again in Jewish writing – to express a thought of such daring novelty that his hearers or readers would have been bound to demand an explanation. Hence the connecting particle that follows: γάρ, 'for'. Both the context and the grammar show that the next sentence, recalling a recent and traumatic incident in his life, is intended to offer some explanation of the surprising language that has just been used.

'For we do not want you to be ignorant, my brothers, of the tribulation we endured in Asia.' In the modern reader, this simply arouses curiosity. We wait with impatience to know what had happened. But we have seen that in their time Paul's words would have been received differently. The question would have been, not, 'In what way were you hurt?' but, 'How serious was it? Was it such as to cause a crisis in your faith?' And this is in fact the question to which Paul's next words are addressed:

> We were excessively afflicted, yes even beyond our powers of resistance, so that we despaired of remaining alive. (AT)

As we shall see in a moment, it is these last words, 'we despaired of remaining alive', which are the significant ones, and which point to something radically unexpected in Paul's experiences. Their importance is confirmed by the fact that it is only they, in this entire passage of personal autobiography, that cannot be paralleled in the literature from which Paul undoubtedly drew the language to describe these experiences: the Psalms. Psalm 38 (37 LXX) describes the 'weight' of sin by which the sufferer felt himself oppressed[42] – the same word (θλίπτειν) as is here translated 'afflicted'. Psalm 116 (114 and 115 LXX) contains many of the key words that Paul uses in the sentences that follow.[43] That is to say, it is not just as a man of his time that Paul showed so little interest in recounting the circumstances of his suffering. It is also as a man of prayer, a man who prayed constantly in the traditional words of the psalms and who naturally adopted the psalmist's manner of interpreting his experience in terms of a recognition of past sinfulness, a protestation of present innocence, and a conviction of the ultimate justification and salvation that would be granted by God. The resources of this traditional spirituality were available to Paul, as to any pious Jew or Gentile sympathizer, to describe, interpret and surmount those trials and tribulations which he could believe were in accordance with God's will for him. Yet when the crisis turned so severe that the sufferer was faced with imminent

---

[42] Ps. 37.5 LXX: 'My transgressions have weighed upon me like a heavy burden.' This is more likely to be in Paul's mind than the image of an overloaded ship (Martin, 14), though the same image could of course be suggested by the word 'burden' (φόρτιον = freight) in the psalm.

[43] Ps. 114 LXX. 3, θλῖψις, 4 ῥῦσαι, 6 ἐταπεινώθην (cf. 115.1), 8 ἐκ θανάτου ('affliction', 'rescue', 'humiliation', 'from death').

death, the shock was such that piety and poetry no longer sufficed, and Paul had to resort to blunt description: 'We despaired of remaining alive.'

I shall give reasons shortly for the importance which I believe must be ascribed to these words. But first we must complete our study of the context in which they occur and then return to the question, which we cannot leave entirely open, of what had happened to bring Paul to such a moment of despair. Paul continues:

> Indeed we felt in our hearts that we had received a death sentence.
> This was meant to teach us to place reliance, not on ourselves, but on God who raises the dead. (1.9)

It is instructive to compare this with Paul's account in Philippians of another experience which brought him very close to death (Phil. 1.21ff.). But this time he seems to have, in some measure, kept the initiative himself. Whether he died or not apparently depended on his own decision: 'Which then am I to choose? I cannot tell.' (Phil. 1.22).[44] That is a very different matter from believing that he 'had received a death sentence'[45] from which only a more or less miraculous intervention by God (in this case assisted by the prayers of the faithful) could rescue him. It is this frank confession that Paul had been brought to the point of accepting the virtual inevitability of death that allows us, finally, to say something about the nature of 'the tribulation we endured in Asia'.

We have seen that the words that Paul used of it ('tribulation', 'excessively afflicted') do not in themselves yield any clear evidence. The first was more often used of persecution, the second of illness; but neither is precise enough to sustain a decision between one and the other. We have seen also that other references to a similar crisis are equally ambivalent: the 'thorn in the flesh' could have been a nagging opponent as much as a chronic disease, and the reference to 'eyes' in

---

[44] For a plausible account of the reason why the issue of life and death could in fact have been in Paul's hands, see J.-F. Collange, *L'Épître de St Paul aux Philippiens* (Neuchâtel, 1973) 26: Paul was faced with the question whether or not to reveal his Roman citizenship.

[45] The interpretation of ἀπόκριμα is keenly disputed (Martin, 15–16, lists five possibilities); but it certainly implies a threat of death outside Paul's control.

Galatians could be no more than a figure of speech. On the other hand we have seen reason to think that the words, 'we despaired of remaining alive', should be taken literally. At this stage in the letter he is not responding to criticism or engaging in polemics. He is simply telling the Corinthians of the desperate condition from which he has been miraculously delivered. He has no reason to exaggerate: we can take his word for it that something brought him to the very point of death.

This excludes at once certain possibilities. 'Persecution', as such, could hardly have had this consequence. It is conceivable that his opponents attempted to murder him and left him with a nearly fatal wound; but the kind of persecution we hear about, however unpleasant, usually takes a less drastic form. More probable is some kind of critical illness that could have arisen from natural causes or else, more probably, have been precipitated by the extreme hardships he had endured – particularly, perhaps, the series of severe floggings, any one of which would have tested the resistance of any but the strongest constitution.[46] In any case, as we have seen, Paul had no interest in relating the details; the important thing, and the thing he was keen to tell the Corinthians, was that he had been reduced to a physical condition in which he had to come to terms with the prospect of imminent death. Up to a certain point this experience could be integrated into his traditional Jewish spirituality and expressed in the familiar language of the psalms. But for Paul it had gone considerably beyond that point and precipitated a crisis for which a new language and new spiritual resources were necessary. We shall see that this provides a key to some profound perceptions that come to light later in the letter. But first we need to take account of the immediate consequences that such an experience would have had for Paul's social life, his reputation and his religious faith.

'We despaired of remaining alive.'

Even if we know nothing of the circumstances which led to the crisis, we can at least say this: Paul must have been severely incapacitated

---

[46] The Mishnah (Mak. 3.14) allows for the possibility that it might result in death.

for a certain period. If his very survival was in doubt, his physical
condition must have been precarious and could hardly have allowed a
rapid recovery. For a time, that is to say, he was a sick man; and we
need to take account of the consequences which would have followed.

Let us begin with economics. An immediate consequence of any
severe form of illness was that one was unable to work; and ancient
society provided no support for those suddenly cut off from their
means of livelihood. As Plato said (apparently without irony), only
the rich could afford to be ill.[47] The middle and lower classes, once
unfit for work, had no means of support for themselves and their
families other than the subvention of relatives and (in the case of Jewish
society) the charitable visiting which was one of the works of piety
encouraged by their religion.[48] If the illness persisted, any reserves of
capital would soon be exhausted on doctors' fees (as in the case of the
woman with a haemorrhage in the gospels); after that the only sources
of help were the healing shrines of pagan religion and (in the case of
both Jewish and pagan society) any purveyor of miraculous cures who
might be found within travelling distance – Jesus himself was
approached on many occasions with this in view. If no cure was
obtained and the patient was still unable to work he might be reduced
to begging, of which the social disgrace could be a source of suffering
as keen as the illness itself.[49]

Paul had no family: to this extent the economic consequences of
being incapacitated for work may have been less severe. On the other
hand we know that he took particular pride in his financial
independence. It was a point of honour for him to support himself by
his trade, a style of life for which he was apparently criticized;[50] yet,
though he claimed the right for others to receive financial support in
return for their preaching and pastoral ministry, he consistently refused

---

[47] *Republic* 406 c–e.
[48] 'The economic threat ... of disease to the lower and middle classes was grave, graver
perhaps than at any later time.' E. C. L. Edelstein, *Asclepius* (Baltimore, 1945) 2.175.
[49] On sanctuaries, see G. Theissen, *The Miracle Stories of the Early Christian Tradition*
(Edinburgh, 1983) 235ff. On shrines, magic, sorcery etc. in antiquity, see A. E. Harvey
Jesus and the Constraints of History (London, 1982) ch. 5.
[50] R. F. Hock, *The Social Context of Paul's Ministry* (Philadelphia, 1980) remains the standard
discussion of this.

the same privilege for himself, and regarded it as a point of honour never to be a 'burden' (βάρος) on his congregations. It may be no accident, but rather a natural association of ideas, that causes Paul to use the same word in connection with his own nearly fatal loss of strength and independence: 'We were excessively burdened' (ἐβαρήθημεν). Quite apart from the ordinary economic consequences of any period of severe illness or disability, it had called into question the whole style of life which Paul had proudly claimed for himself as an apostle.

No less serious than the economic consequences were the social ones. Suppose a member of one's circle of friends fell on bad times, lost his reputation or became ill. Again, a family network might rally round, for example, to buy a debtor out of prison. But such things brought discredit on any social group: the assumption – still held, even if almost unconsciously, by all but the most sophisticated people – that illness was a consequence of some form of wrong-doing[51] meant that the sufferer could expect to become something of a pariah.

> My heart throbs, my strength is spent,
> and the light has faded from my eyes.
> My friends and my companions shun me in my sickness,
> and my kinsfolk keep far off. (Ps. 38.10–11)

It is precisely the same predicament that Paul describes in Galatians (4.12–15). Here again, we cannot be sure whether the condition which was afflicting him was the result of disease or of weakness brought on by hardship and persecution. In the context of his argument the latter is perhaps more probable.[52] But in any case he writes that his sickly appearance among the Galatians presented them with a test or temptation (πειρασμός). They might have shunned him as an object-lesson of the physical consequences of exposing themselves to

---

[51] Not only among the Jews: cf. Simonides' 'Pittakos' poem (PMG, 542) – 'it is impossible for a man to be good who is destroyed by an irresistible disaster'.

[52] Persuasively argued for by A. J. Goddard and S. A. Cummins, 'Ill or ill-treated? Conflict and persecution as the context of Paul's original ministry in Galatia (Galatians 4.12–20)' *JSNT* 52 (1993) 93–126, who list (95 n. 7) the commentators, patristic and modern, who support this view.

persecution; they might have written him off (ἐξουθενήσατε) as a failed apostle; they might even have drawn the conclusion that his condition was the result of some form of demon-possession, in which case the appropriate reaction would have been to ward off the danger to themselves by spitting at him (οὐδὲ ἐξεπτύσατε).[53] It was greatly to their credit that they had done none of these things; but the very possibility that they might have done so alerts us to the hostile reaction that any bout of illness or serious physical weakness might provoke; the danger of being banished from his circle of friends was a major part of the distress of a person suddenly struck down with a physical affliction.[54]

It was a danger Paul seems to have had in mind, not only for himself, but for his colleague Epaphroditus, who was 'in great anxiety' (ἀδημονῶν) because it had become known that he was sick (Phil. 2.26). Paul admits that Epaphroditus' illness had been nearly fatal, but explains that it had been brought on by his exertions for the 'work of Christ' (2.30).[55] Why then should Epaphroditus have been so disturbed by the thought of the Philippians knowing about it? Commentators have exercised much ingenuity;[56] but his anxiety becomes intelligible the moment we take seriously the normal social consequences of any near-fatal illness.

But most serious of all were the consequences for a person's self-esteem and religious standing. One must not assume, of course, that the ancients were universally lacking in compassion and sympathy for

---

[53] Seybold and Mueller, op. cit. 172; J. Neyrey, *Paul, in Other Words* (Louisville, 1990) 176–7. This interpretation, advanced by H. Schlier in his commentary (KEK, 1949) and in his article in *TWNT* s.v. ἐκπτύω (1964), has been widely adopted but is criticized by Goddard and Cummins (art. cit. 103–7) for having given insufficient weight to the well-attested metaphorical use of the compounds of πτύω. But they admit that the word always implied scorn or disgust, which is not fully explained by their view that the Galatians saw Paul as an innocent victim of persecution.

[54] K. Seybold, *Das Gebet des Kranken* (see n. 31) 51–3 traces a progression from 'Distanzierung' through 'Isolierung', being treated 'wie ein Fremder', 'Beschimpfung', 'Feindseligkeit' to 'gerichtliche Folgerung'.

[55] So J. B. Lightfoot, *St Paul's Epistle to the Philippians* (London, 1908) 125. The discussion by L. G. Bloomquist, *The Function of Suffering in Philippians, JSNTSS* 78 (Sheffield, 1993), which assumes that Epaphroditus had suffered, not from illness, but from persecution, seems to discount the twice repeated ἠσθένησεν.

[56] E.g. Calvin and Lohmeyer, who suggest that it was prompted by a difficult situation at Philippi.

the victims of illness and misfortune. The merit attached to sick visiting as an act of charity in the Jewish culture is a case in point, even though there were some who felt it inappropriate to do so on the Sabbath for fear of spoiling the general sense of happiness and well-being for which the day was intended.[57] Yet it remains true that both for the philosopher and for the religious thinker sickness remained something of a surd – something that, in theory, should not happen. The whole tendency of Stoic, and still more of Cynic, asceticism was to demonstrate the power of the philosophically trained mind over the weaknesses of the flesh. An unmerited illness seemed to contradict this pretension, and so was banished from serious philosophical discussion. Among the rabbis the problem was taken more seriously. The basic assumption was that illness is the consequence of sin.[58] In theory, therefore, one should be able to gauge the seriousness of the offence by the severity of the physical condition. In many cases we read that this calculus was actually applied.[59] But there were others in which it seemed too implausible to be true, in which case relief was offered by an alternative explanation: God sent the sickness to discipline his elect.[60] Accordingly, a long line of sufferers, from the Psalmist and Job to the subjects of Jesus' exorcisms in the gospels, saw their afflictions as directly related to some flaw in their relationship with God. Any sudden vicissitude would be read as a sign of some new unwitting offence, the recrudescence of some old unhealed rebelliousness or the need for further discipline and purification. The obverse of such self-analysis was of course the opinion of others. If one had doubts oneself about one's own innocence before God, how much more readily might even one's friends entertain the same suspicion, how gleefully might one's enemies exploit the occasion to initiate a campaign of denigration:

> I have become a stranger to my brothers,
> an alien to my mother's sons ...

---

[57] On sick visiting in general, see S-B 4.573–8. The school of Shammai argued against it on the Sabbath, Shab. 12a.
[58] Cf. G. F. Moore, *Judaism* 2 (Harvard, 1927) 246–56.
[59] S-B 2.193–7.
[60] E.g. Ps. Sol. 10.1–3.

Those who sit by the town gate gossip about me;
I am the theme of drunken songs ...
Let me be rescued from my enemies
and from the watery depths. (Ps. 69.8, 12, 14)

It required both an unshakable confidence in one's own innocence
and an aggressive campaign to scotch the suspicions of friends and
the insinuations of enemies to put out of court the usual inferences
that would be drawn from such an apparently tell-tale reversal of
fortune.

It is precisely this combination of protestations of innocence, appeals
to the better judgment of friends and ironic comment on the alleged
success and well-being of his opponents that characterizes much of
Paul's writing in 2 Corinthians. For this purpose he found a vocabulary
and a store of images to hand in those of the psalms that express a
similar crisis of faith, psalms which we can assume were one of the
main resources of his own spiritual life and of which the Greek version
has left evident traces in his writing.[61] To take only one example: Psalm
118.17–18 (117.17 in the Greek) reads

I shall not die but I shall live
and recite the words of the Lord.
With discipline the Lord disciplined me (ἐπαίδευσεν)
yet he did not hand me over to death.

2 Corinthians 6.9 echoes the same phrases:

Dying we still live on;
disciplined by suffering (παιδευόμενοι)
we are not done to death.

Here Paul resorts to one of the traditional means of coming to terms
with apparently undeserved suffering: it is sent even to the good man
as a form of discipline. But more typical of the thrust of the whole

---

[61] Helpfully discussed by Frances Young in F. Young and D. F. Ford, *Meaning and Truth in
2 Corinthians* (London, 1987) ch. 3.

letter is the sense of deliverance as an endorsement of the sufferer's rectitude and as a decisive refutation of the charges against him, such as is expressed in Psalm 41.11–12:

> Then shall I know that you delight in me
> and that my enemy will not triumph over me.
> But I am upheld by you because of my innocence;
> You keep me for ever in your presence.

Here, the threat that an illness or a major reversal of fortune poses to a man of faith and piety receives eloquent expression. And the sense that the only remedy is trust in God –

> On you Lord I fix my hope;
> You, Lord my God, will answer. (Ps. 38.15) –

determines the way in which Paul describes his own deliverance from a nearly fatal condition:

> This was to teach us to place reliance not on
> ourselves, but on God who raises the dead.
> From such mortal peril God delivered us;
> and he will deliver us again, he on whom our hope is fixed.
> (2 Cor. 1.9–10)

Yet even this is not all. In Paul's case there was a further factor. In 1 Thessalonians (his earliest surviving letter) Paul had written,

> Those of us who are still alive when the Lord comes
> will have no advantage over those who have died ...
> First the Christian dead will rise,
> then we who are still alive shall join them,
> caught up in clouds to meet the Lord in the air. (4.15–17)

Clearly it had not crossed his mind that he might not be alive himself on the day of Christ's glorious return; and the same confidence is still apparent in 1 Corinthians:

We shall not all die, but we shall all be changed ...
the dead will rise imperishable, and we shall be changed.

(15.51–2)

Some Christians, admittedly, had already died or might still die before
that day, some from natural causes and therefore 'dead in Christ'
(1 Thess. 4.16; cf. 1 Cor. 15.23), some having brought on their own
death by failing to discern the body of Christ in the eucharist (1 Cor.
11.29–30). But the majority would be alive; and there can be no doubt
that, at least up to the time of writing 1 Corinthians, Paul reckoned
himself among them.

It is against this background of confident personal expectation that
we need to measure the impact of an experience which caused Paul to
write, only a few months later, that he 'despaired even of remaining
alive'. We can infer that it was a profound shock, not only to his own
perception of his personal destiny, but – and this may have been more
traumatic – to his status in the eyes of others; one who had always
claimed to be in the vanguard of those who would be alive to greet the
risen Christ when he returned in glory had been shown to be as
vulnerable as anyone else to the threat of untimely death. This is not
to say that he was led to change his view on the imminence of the
Lord's coming. Even if by this time there may have been some
slackening of the tension of expectation in the church – and it is not
easy to prove that there was – Paul continued to alert his readers to
the need to be prepared: 'Deliverance is nearer to us now than it was
when first we believed'; 'The Lord is near' – these sentences come
from Romans (13.11) and Philippians (4.5), both of which were
certainly written later than 2 Corinthians. In the face of these, it is
hardly plausible to argue that Paul was ceasing to take seriously the
imminent prospect of Christ's return. But what must have changed,
and changed radically, was his own personal expectation of being alive
to see it. The point had evidently not escaped his critics either, who
were now accusing him of preaching his message from doubtful motives
and inferring that he had something serious on his conscience.

If, then, we are right in thinking that 'the tribulation which came
upon us in Asia' involved a period of severe physical weakness,
dependence and incapacity for work, the consequences for Paul will

have been extremely serious. In terms of physical survival, he will have temporarily lost the independence he set such store by, and will have owed his recovery to the devotion and material support of others. In terms of social status and reputation, he is likely to have received rebuffs and discouragement. With regard to his work and achievements, his condition will have given rise to suspicions and accusations of dishonesty and duplicity; and as for his own confidence and sense of vocation, he will have had to come to terms with an experience of near-fatal suffering which seemed to contradict both his self-understanding as one appointed by God to preach the gospel throughout the Gentile world and his natural expectation of being one of those who would be alive when Christ returned in glory. Once he was safely over it, Paul will have been keen to reassure the Corinthians and thank them for their prayers. But he evidently had other reasons for giving it such a prominent place at the beginning of his letter. He needed to assure his readers that none of the suspicions and criticisms that the episode had given rise to had any basis in fact. More important, he was keen to impart something of his own experience, which had enabled him to reconcile this extreme and nearly fatal 'tribulation' with his self-understanding as a chosen apostle of Christ and had opened up for him, and so for others, a new way of coming to terms with suffering itself. This was the thrust of the 'consolation' – which, as we have seen, includes also the sense of 'encouragement' – which he had received and which he felt able to communicate to other Christians who might be faced with a comparable tribulation.

It was also, I believe, a major discovery in its own right. Paul had endured an experience that seemed at odds with all that he believed, shattering for his own self-confidence and challenging the very basis of his Christian faith. It was the problem of evil suddenly presented in its most acute and apparently inexplicable form. What resources were available to him to surmount it? There were, first, the stock explanations of suffering which were common currency in his own religious tradition. 'These things are sent to try us' – we have seen that Paul was prepared to accept this explanation up to a point; but the more general and popular assumption that such afflictions were a symptom of undisclosed wrong-doing he resisted with absolute conviction, aligning

himself with Job and the psalmist and all other sufferers whose
conscience told them they had done nothing to deserve such an
affliction. There was also a philosophical type of answer,[62] going back
ultimately to Socrates and much in favour with stoic and cynic teachers,
who would present an impressive catalogue of the vicissitudes they
had been through in order to show how the sage can achieve
indifference to a daunting range of physical and mental sufferings.
This again was something Paul could draw on; indeed it is even possible
that the later (and historically quite unreliable) accounts we have of
Paul's appearance are a reflection of this attitude.[63] 'Bald, bow-legged,
with meeting eyebrows and hooked nose' – this unattractive picture is
often thought to be an attempt to play down his physical appearance
in the interests of enhancing his spiritual virtues; but in fact it may be
a deliberate idealization, in terms of a heroic Hercules (the type so
dear to Cynic propaganda) whose prowess is displayed in almost
supernatural feats of indifference to the temptations and weaknesses
of the body – though if Paul made conscious use of this kind of
argument he will have been careful to avoid anything that seemed like
boasting of his own personal self-discipline and philosophical detachment:
the credit must go, not to himself, but to a higher power within him.

Paul undoubtedly drew on these traditional resources – we shall
find examples at many points in the letter – but were they sufficient
to explain the extreme of apparently meaningless suffering he had just
endured? The trials of the righteous might be endurable so long as
some relief could be hoped for: anyone who regularly used the psalms
for his prayers could find reassurance to that extent. The trials of the
sage could be a helpful example of philosophical endurance so long as
he was not actually overwhelmed by them. But suppose life itself was
threatened. Suppose (to use and extend Paul's own figure of speech)
the earthenware vessel was not just chipped and cracked but actually
broken – a prospect Paul had suddenly had to face: what then? In a
moment of such darkness the consolations of philosophy, the theory
of divine chastisement or the testing and refining of the spirit through

---

[62] This is set out in detail in his study of the *Peristasen* catalogues by J. Fitzgerald, *Cracks in
an Earthen Vessel* (see above, n. 38).

[63] This is argued by A. J. Malherbe, 'A Physical Description of Paul' *HTR* 79 (1986) 170–
75 = *Paul and the Popular Philosophers* (Minneapolis, 1989) 165–70.

suffering, are hopelessly inadequate. The sufferer longs to find some meaning in a human condition which philosophical and religious thinkers could only treat as negative, as an affliction to be surmounted through self-discipline or accepted with resignation. This episode in Paul's life had been such as to force him to press the question of suffering beyond any point that had been reached, I believe, by the most reflective of his contemporaries.[64]

There was of course one approach that was opened up by the Christian (and, in certain circles, the Jewish) belief in the resurrection. This is well illustrated in 1 Corinthians 15, where Paul, in a somewhat rhetorical style, advances a number of reasons for regarding the resurrection of the dead as an absolutely vital article of belief, without which we would be the most miserable of human beings. To clinch the argument, he writes

And why do we ourselves face danger hour by hour? …
With no more than human hopes, what would have been
the point of my fighting those wild beasts at Ephesus?
If the dead are never raised to life, 'Let us eat and
drink, for tomorrow we die'. (1 Cor. 15.30–32)

Fighting with wild beasts at Ephesus is hardly to be taken literally: those who were forced to do so in a Roman arena did not normally live to tell the tale! More likely it is an expression derived, once again, from the repertoire of the Cynic sage,[65] who prided himself on subduing his passions and physical discomforts as Hercules overcame the wild beasts in his path. At any rate, the sense of the passage is clear: without a firm hope of recompense after resurrection, what would be the point of enduring afflictions here and now? For the Christian, the key to

---

[64] The suffering and death of the Maccabean martyrs is accounted for in 2 and 4 Maccabees as providing an outstanding example of endurance 'for the sake of the law' (2 Macc. 6.28, 31; 4 Macc. 7.8). But there is no trace in 2 Corinthians of Paul having tried to understand his own sufferings in these martyrological terms. See the study of this question by D. Seeley, *The Noble Death, JSNT*SS 28 (Sheffield, 1990), who seems not to distinguish sufficiently between the 'mimetic' value of suffering (inspiring others with courage and reason to suffer) and the 'vicarious' value (suffering *in place of* others).

[65] A. J. Malherbe, 'The Beasts of Ephesus', *JBL* 87 (1968) 71–80 = *Paul and the Popular Philosophers* 79–90.

the problem of suffering in the present is the promise of a compensating reward in the future.

When he wrote 1 Corinthians, therefore, Paul still shared the general supposition of his contemporaries that suffering is a purely negative experience. It may be a necessary discipline or chastisement imposed by God; it may be a school or contest in which the sage may cultivate a philosophical detachment; it may be just a more or less inexplicable deprivation of normal well-being that a Christian may believe will be abundantly made good by God in the afterlife. If we now compare what Paul says on the subject in 2 Corinthians – possibly only a few months later, but after the traumatic experience described at the outset – the contrast is startling. For the first time in his extant letters, and possibly for the first time in the entire philosophical and religious literature of the West, we find the experience of involuntary and innocent suffering invested with positive value and meaning *in itself.* The discovery inspires the radically new concepts of 'carrying about the corpse-like condition of Christ' as a means of imparting life, and of the inner man being 'renewed' by the disfigurement and decay of the outer man, that are worked out in 2 Corinthians 4; it underlies other striking expressions elsewhere, such as 'filling up in one's own flesh the tale of Christ's sufferings' (Col. 1.24, which we may safely assume was a later writing). It seems that this unprecedented recognition of the positive value of suffering for the Christian, suffering that can be shared with Christ in a new and intimate solidarity, was forced upon Paul by an episode in his own life. This episode presented him with the problem of suffering in its sharpest form. In a moment when he was led to 'despair even of remaining alive' he was faced by the apparent destruction of his self-confidence, his hopes and his credibility in the eyes of others. None of the received philosophical and religious explanations was adequate for coping with such a crisis. Instead, Paul found his way to a perception of the spiritual strengths and riches that a Christian may experience in circumstances of utter dereliction through solidarity with Christ. It is a perception that has been endorsed again and again in the experience of Christians down the centuries; but I believe it was first discovered and tested, and then received rich theological expression, as a result of the experience Paul felt impelled to impart to his readers, when he had 'despaired even of remaining alive'.

Chapter 2

The Aftermath

2 Corinthians 1.10–4.6

Paul tells us as little about his recovery as he does about the circumstances of his 'near-death' experience. Once again, the key to this reticence is not to be found in any personal evasiveness but in the strength of the cultural tradition which provided the appropriate conventions and vocabulary. The sufferer in the psalms wastes no words on the favourable circumstances of rest or diet, or the devoted nursing and encouragement of relatives and friends, which may have contributed to his recovery. All the emphasis is on prayer, the 'rescue' afforded by God, and the thanksgiving this evokes:

> I love the Lord, for he has heard me
> and listened to my prayer ...
> I invoked the Lord by name,
> 'Lord, deliver me, I pray' ...
> When I was brought low, he saved me ...
> You have rescued me from death ...
> I shall pay my vows to the Lord
> in the presence of all his people. (Ps. 116. 1, 4–7, 18)

So with Paul: the word used for 'deliver' in the Greek version of the psalm (114.4 LXX) – ῥῦσαι – occurs no less than three times in the brief passage in which Paul ascribes his recovery to the intervention of God and the prayers of his friends (1.10–11).

But, rather than stay with this mood of thankful recollection, Paul immediately moves to another topic related to it – his *pride*. The Greek word καύχησις, like its English equivalent, usually had a negative connotation: any expression of 'pride' in one's own achievements offended against traditional Greek standards of a proper deference towards the uncertainty of the future and the unpredictable favours of the gods,[1] and any show of philosophical detachment from adversity was felt to be rendered false and valueless if the philosopher began to pride himself on it.[2] When recounting the troubles he had undergone for the sake of his religion, Paul was going to have to be watchful to avoid any suspicion of boasting of his own endurance. But at the same time, in the culture of Greek-speaking Jews, the word could have a more positive connotation. The dangers of a normally sinful or imprudent 'pride' need not be present if it was what we might call a 'proper pride', or a legitimate 'confidence' provided by someone or something else.[3] For this, the same Greek word could be used; and it may have been this very ambiguity of the word, its range of meanings from 'boasting' on the one hand to 'serene confidence' on the other, that invited Paul to make such subtle use of it. In the course of 2 Corinthians he uses it, or some form of it, no less than twenty-seven times – there are not more instances in the whole of the rest of the New Testament. He was well aware (he tells us so himself)[4] of the danger of 'pride' in his own case: he could all too easily be accused of having tried to take credit for his own survival – this would have been a natural reaction to the lack of credibility to which he was exposed through his reverses and sufferings. But this did not prevent there being a genuine 'proper pride' which lay at the root of Paul's own religious experience.

Since the term occurs so frequently, and with such emphasis, in his letter, it is important to ask exactly what Paul means by it. We may note, in the first place, that he uses the word in an entirely positive sense. In chapters 11 and 12 his καύχησις may certainly sound like boasting, and he is aware that he has to guard himself against criticism. But here, any boastful connotation of the word 'pride' is purged by its subject: the grace of God, manifested in

---

[1] Though of course a 'proper pride' was in order. See above, p. 15 n. 38.

[2] Epict. *Diss.* 4.8.27–29.

[3] Prov. 17.6; Ps. 88.17 LXX. Cf. the exhaustive discussion in U. Heckel, *Kraft in Schwachheit* WUNT 56 (Tübingen, 1993) 144–214, who finds the key in Jer. 9.23 LXX.

[4] E.g. 2 Cor. 10.8.

simplicity and transparency of character (1.12). This confident or proper pride is that recommended by the psalmist: 'Be confident (καυχᾶσθε), all who are upright of heart' (Ps. 31.11 LXX); 'all those who love your name will have confidence in you' (Ps. 5.12 LXX). And it is Paul's 'conscience' that assures him that this is the nature of his own confidence. He is not taking credit for anything other than the evidence afforded by his own life that God does indeed accept and support him.

This, then, is the proper way to receive Paul's announcement of his deliverance and recovery: not as self-congratulation on his stamina and resources of stoical detachment, but as a celebration of God's goodness and an acknowledgement of the prayers that have been said for him. But there is a significant addition to this simple, biblical thought. Paul's 'conduct in the world' has been

in the simplicity and sincerity of God,
not in natural ('fleshly') wisdom but in the grace of God. (1.12) AT

Paul helps us to determine the character of his true conduct by invoking its opposite: 'fleshly wisdom'. By calling wisdom 'fleshly' he is clearly referring to something undesirable; and this, on the face of it, is a highly paradoxical expression. 'Wisdom' was normally something that was wholly good. In Greek, as in English, it was a virtue that combined intelligence with sound judgement and moral integrity, indeed it was the very goal and achievement of philosophy. In the Jewish tradition, likewise, it was God's gift to the greatest sages and was an aspect of God's creative power, the source of order and regularity in the universe. How could Paul denigrate it to the extent of describing it by the evidently pejorative word 'fleshly'? It was true, of course, that in Christ Paul believed there was now manifested a greater wisdom, or (to put it another way) that it was only in Christ that the true nature of God's wisdom had at last been revealed. This new revelation relativized all previous perceptions of wisdom and made it possible to describe them as 'the wisdom of this world' as opposed to the true wisdom now revealed in Christ. But this 'worldly wisdom', though now superseded by a superior wisdom, did not thereby become invalid or disreputable: Paul continued to make use of 'wisdom' maxims alongside his new-

found Christian perceptions;[5] the inheritance of the wisdom embodied
in Scripture and the sanctified common sense of a long line of religious
teachers was not to be suddenly discarded, and Paul could certainly
not have been criticized when he continued to use it. When, therefore,
he contrasts the simplicity and sincerity of his conduct with 'fleshly
wisdom' we have to look for another nuance of the word that will give
point to his self-defence.

The nuance we require is in fact at the heart of Paul's argument in
his previous letter to the Corinthians. There, he is defending the
manner and style of his original preaching in Corinth against the
criticism that he lacked the appropriate rhetorical skill. This he fully
concedes: the force and validity of his message lay in its spiritual power,
not in 'persuasive words of wisdom' (2.4); his preaching was not
accomplished by means of 'wise and skilful speech'. The use of 'wisdom'
(σοφία) in that passage is a clear reference to a question that was
constantly raised by the enormous importance and popularity of
rhetorical skills in the Greco–Roman world. Plato had made a clear
distinction between the perfect knowledge of the truth which was the
goal of philosophy (wisdom, σοφία) and the means (rhetoric) by which
it was conveyed to others. The burden of his attack on the 'sophists'
was that they were blurring this distinction and allowing the manner
of their argumentation to seem more important than its truth.[6] The
debate continued down the centuries: philosophers continued to insist
on the distinction between form and content in oratory, but in practice
the two were impossible to keep separate.[7] The 'wisdom' of orators
seemed to be inextricably bound up with their skills of persuasion,
and these, since they could in principle be enlisted to advance any
cause whatever (as in the law courts) and by no means depended for
their effect on the truth of the case being advanced, were regarded
with suspicion by people in search of the ultimate truth about God
and humanity. If Paul was being criticized for his lack of these skills, it
was entirely proper for him to reply that the possession of them would

---

[5] See the discussion in A. E. Harvey, *Strenuous Commands: the Ethic of Jesus* (London,
      1990) 151–3.
[6] E.g. *Phaedrus* 277e.
[7] For an excellent account, see Duane Litfin, *St Paul's Theology of Proclamation*, 119–24.

have weakened rather than strengthened the force of his preaching. Its persuasiveness depended, not on rhetorical skills, but on the power of God's spirit.

It is precisely this sense of 'wisdom' (σοφία) that is required in 2 Corinthians 1.12 – 'rhetorical skill'.[8] God's wisdom now manifested in Christ may be superior to 'worldly wisdom', but it does not make 'worldly wisdom' (the maxims by which a wise person lives) in any way disreputable. That Paul showed himself 'wise' in this sense would hardly be something he felt it necessary to deny. On the other hand, the suggestion that he was making use of rhetorical skills is one that he might well have wished to repudiate, since he had distanced himself from any such accomplishments on a previous occasion. True, on that occasion he had been criticized (it seems) for *not* having these skills. Why should he now have to counter the suggestion that he had them? The clue lies in the general suspicion of rhetoric that was shared by philosophers and religious people:[9] if a man was a trained and skilful public speaker, how could you be sure that he was telling the truth? Paul's concern now was to demonstrate his simplicity and sincerity: any suggestion that he had been resorting to the technical skills of persuasive rhetoric would have damaged his case.

But we still have to ask why anyone might have thought of criticizing him on these grounds when not many months previously he had been charged with *lack* of skill in rhetoric – a charge which is heard again later in 2 Corinthians (11.6). To which the answer must be that if Paul had to insist that he had been entirely straightforward and sincere in his conduct, and was innocent of any *double entendre* in the letters he wrote (1.13), then the argument of his critics must have been that Paul had been resorting, however crudely, to rhetorical techniques in order to press his case and cover up the truth. If the essence of rhetoric was to make a poor case seem more plausible and a weak position more credible, then the imputation that Paul had been trying to make use of such skills would amount to saying that his words were not to be believed.

---

8   As in e.g. Dio Chrys. *Or.* 42.5, where σοφία is clearly 'skill' as much as 'wisdom'. Cf. *Or.* 77.1f.

9   Cf. Philo *Vit.Cont.* 75.

But at what point would such a criticism have struck home? What would have laid Paul open to the charge that he was dissembling, that he lacked credibility and that he was resorting to the techniques of 'fleshly wisdom' to cover up the truth? There are far too many gaps in our knowledge of Paul's dealings with the Corinthians for us to be sure of the answer. But the immediate context of this short defence of his sincerity suggests one very plausible explanation. Paul has just referred to the experience which nearly caused his death and from which he had made a miraculous recovery. We have seen that one consequence of this experience is likely to have been a serious loss of credibility as an authorized apostle of Christ, as the preacher of a gospel of salvation and as a member of that privileged band of followers who would be alive at the return of the Lord. Those who had believed him before might well have their doubts now, and come to suspect that his former protestations of a transparently clear conscience were an instance of 'fleshly wisdom', the use of rhetorical persuasion to strengthen a fundamentally weak case. This is the supposition that Paul is so anxious to deny.

'In this confidence I desired to come to you first ...' (1.15). 'Confidence' again: not the same word as before (καύχησις) but one with an almost identical meaning (πεποίθησις); evidently the course Paul wanted to adopt was one that would not have been open to him had he not been convinced both that his own motives were pure and that there was no serious risk of him being misunderstood. What was this project, and why was there an element of risk in it? A few verses later Paul is explaining why he subsequently had to change his plans; and ever since John Chrysostom[10] commentators have jumped to the conclusion that the critics against whom Paul was defending himself were attacking him for his unreliability: after announcing his plans, he thought nothing of altering them, he was notoriously 'fickle' (1.17). But before we are swept along by this facile explanation there are some points in the text to be noted which suggest that the true explanation may be elsewhere.

(i)   The traditional view presupposes that it was Paul's subsequent change of plan – his failure to make the promised second visit to

---

[10] Chrys. ad loc. (BP p. 37).

Corinth – which was the object of criticism. But there is not a word here about the way his plans turned out: these verses (15–22) are entirely devoted to his original wishes and intentions – 'I wanted to come to you … when I *wanted* this was I being "fickle"? Were my *plans* "fleshly" …?' It seems that Paul had to defend himself against charges that he had done wrong even before he was forced to change his plans: it was the original project that aroused criticism.

(ii)   In verse 15 there is an enigmatic phrase, 'so that you should have a second favour'. Given that Paul goes on to talk about making two visits to Corinth, one before and one after his journey north to Macedonia, it has seemed natural to assume that the 'second favour' refers to the second of these visits. But it has to be admitted (as most commentators recognize) that this would be an odd way of putting it:[11] 'I wanted to come to you first (i.e. before going to Macedonia) in order that you should have a second visit after I came back from Macedonia.' A far more natural way of taking it is as a reference to Paul's *next* visit to Corinth – 'I wanted to give you a favour again (i.e. a second favour) by coming.' In which case, what was the first 'favour'? It is possible that Paul meant his first and original visit to Corinth, when he stayed nearly two years and certainly supported himself (so that his stay was 'gratis'); or he may have been referring to a subsequent visit which had been painful in certain respects but may also have been without charge, and so a 'favour'.[12] But in either case the reference would be to a visit Paul had in fact already paid; there ceases to be any mention in this whole paragraph of anything which could be called a change of plan, or about which Paul could have been criticized as having been 'fickle'.

(iii)   'With this intention was I showing my (well-known) fickleness (ἐλαφρία)?' (1.17). It is along these lines that translators have rendered

---

[11] Windisch attributes it to 'the haste of dictation', 63.

[12] It is important to notice that the *only* evidence for this 'painful visit', or for any visit between the writing of 1 Cor. and 2 Cor. is the phrase, τὸ μὴ παλιν ἐν λύπῃ πρὸς ὑμᾶς ἐλθεῖν (2.1). This may more naturally mean, 'not to make a second painful visit'; but we cannot altogether exclude the meaning, 'not to make another visit which, this time, would be painful'.

this verse at least since the time of St Jerome.[13] But is this what the Greek word ἐλαφρία meant? It is a rare word, and in every case its meaning – other than the purely literal one of physical 'lightness' – is stupidity, irresponsibility. Is it possible that translators and commentators have read into the word a meaning derived from their understanding of this passage? They have assumed that Paul was being criticized for changing his plans, that is, for his unreliability, his 'fickleness'; so that is what he must have meant by his 'lightness'. But if the matter of Paul's change of mind is not the subject of this paragraph at all, but rather something to do with his original intention, we need to look at the question afresh.

We must first take full account of the article: τῇ ἐλαφρίᾳ. This is what the grammarians call 'anaphoric', that is, it refers to something we know already. At the risk of over-translating, we have to say something like 'my well-known ἐλαφρία'. In which case, what does ἐλαφρία mean? It is possible that Paul was well known for changing his mind in an apparently irresponsible way; but we have no other evidence to support the idea. On the other hand, there is one area in which we know that he was extremely sensitive, and subjected to frequent criticism. This was his deliberate policy of making no charge on the local church for the expenses of his stay. For this, at times, he was criticized, as if by refusing his keep he was implicitly conceding that he did not have the authority of a real apostle. But he was also – and this is the relevant point here – disbelieved and suspected of exacting money covertly from his converts or even tampering with the money collected for Jerusalem. Here, then, was a real challenge to his purity of motive. Could this have been the target of criticism here?

To answer this we must pick up two further clues. First, this 'second favour'. Why does Paul refer to a visit in such an indirect way? Early scribes or editors found this difficult, and altered the word χάριν to χαράν, 'joy'.[14] Χάρις means favour, something given gratis and creating no obligation, and it was precisely this 'gratis' character of his mission that Paul prided himself on and worked hard to maintain. His

[13] *Levitas* Vg, cf. Esther 16.9; Tobit 3.17 Vg.
[14] A poorly attested reading, accepted by Plummer and Von Soden against the general consensus of commentators.

intention, then, was to come to Corinth and stay with the Christians there both on his way to and on his way from Macedonia, without making a charge on their hospitality. If, now, he had recently suffered a debilitating illness or an attack so crippling that he nearly died, this would have seemed to others to have been an almost laughable ambition. He could well have been accused of irresponsibility, foolishness, from the moment he began to entertain such a notion. This would give to ἐλαφρία the meaning which the word seems usually to have borne, 'foolish irresponsibility'.[15]

(iii)   Paul gives further precision to the criticism being made of him: his plans involve him in saying 'yes yes' and 'no no'. It is important to be clear about what sort of criticism this could have been. We may say 'yes' or 'no' on all sorts of occasions, many of them trivial.[16] On this occasion Paul is alleged to have said it emphatically (yes, yes; no, no): it was evidently one on which his reply *mattered*. In the context of laying plans this clearly implies *negotiation*: he would accept some conditions, decline others. He might, for example, have said 'yes' in response to an invitation to stay, 'no' to the question whether (as previously) he would pay his own expenses. We cannot, of course, do more than guess at what was the subject of negotiation; what we can say is that *any* such negotiation would have been contrary to Paul's declared intention to pay a visit gratis (a 'favour'). Now that the Corinthians knew that in his present enfeebled condition he could not do this, they might well suspect him of having some *arrière pensée* or hidden agenda, and of intending to negotiate his keep with them when he arrived.

'Our λόγος towards you is not "yes" and "no".' Λόγος, of course, means speech or message; and so it is usually translated. But it also

---

[15]   This is the meaning in all the patristic instances in PGL. It is also the only meaning allowed for by the lexicographers, apart from a mysterious entry in Hesychius: ὀλιγότης. It is however possible that Paul's use of the word has a further nuance. ἐλαφρός, ἐλαφρίζειν were used in connection with 'lightening' taxation. Paul prided himself on not placing a βάρος on his churches by letting them contribute to his needs. Was this his 'well-known ἐλαφρία', which was now no longer seeming credible?

[16]   For an analysis of different degrees of seriousness, and of the importance of the words in negotiation, see J. D. M. Derrett '"ναί" (2 Cor. 1.19–20)', Filologia Neotestamentaria (Cordoba) 8 (1991) 205–9.

means 'reckoning' or 'account' – which is how Paul uses it twice over in the tortuous passage in Philippians (4.14–19) in which, again, he describes the financial independence that was secured for him in Thessalonica by gifts from Philippi. This sense is entirely pertinent here: a 'reckoning' that was 'yes' and 'no' would be a good way of describing a budget which assumed some expenses being paid by the Corinthians. By contrast, the act of God in sending his son Jesus Christ involved no such calculation of profit and loss, no 'yes' and 'no' in response to different possibilities: it was pure 'favour', grace.

It may be felt that all this is reading between the lines: if Paul was really talking about money all the time, why did he not say so? But in fact this was a matter on which Paul was extremely sensitive. In the passage from Philippians which I have just referred to, he goes to extraordinary lengths to avoid having to speak directly about money – as is often the case among friends: we are embarrassed to mention the payments we owe to or expect from one another, and prefer to hint at them obliquely. If Paul's real anxiety here was (as I have suggested) that he feared that his recent inability to fend for himself would raise doubts about whether he ever intended to do so, and whether therefore his word was to be believed, it would be entirely characteristic of him to express himself with an allusive complexity which, ever since, his interpreters have found 'hard to understand' (2 Peter 3.16).

The complexity is of course increased by the fact that, as so often, Paul makes a theological point out of something that would normally be dealt with on a practical or moral level.[17] The question raised matters of motive and conscience: had Paul made plans that were beyond his abilities to fulfil? Would he be involved in negotiations with the Corinthians that would be hard to reconcile with his professed intention to be doing them a 'favour' by making a visit altogether free of charge? His answer was to show that this was a false interpretation of events; but there was a further dimension. Paul's entire energies were devoted to proclaiming the message of God's free gift to humankind in Christ Jesus. This was God's 'grace' or 'favour'. It was

[17] A. E. Harvey, 'The Opposition to Paul', SE 4 (1968) 319–332 at p. 332.

essential to this message that God must never be thought of as 'making terms'. God had made promises to his people in the past: a notable one was that described in Jeremiah 31.31–4, of a new covenant and a law to be written in the heart. But the people's response to this had never been an unqualified 'yes'; they had never been willing to take on unreservedly the obligations towards God that this implied; they had said (in effect), 'yes, but also no'. It was only Christ who had given unqualified assent, who had said 'yes' to God without any trace of 'no'.[18] And this 'yes' – expressed in worship as '*amen*' – was now expressed in the life of Christ's followers, that is, people whom God had 'anointed and sealed' and empowered by the Spirit to experience some anticipation of that perfect obedience (1.21–22). It was essential to the proclamation of the gospel that the same unqualified 'yes' should characterize all the conduct of those who preached it.

Up to this point, then, this whole paragraph has been concerned with *plans*: whether Paul had been justified in making them, what his motives were, and whether they were consistent with his professed policies and motives and indeed with the message he proclaimed of a God who had been totally generous in his gift of his son Jesus Christ and who demanded a totally single-minded response from his followers. Only now does Paul turn to the fact that these plans were not in fact carried out. Once again we note an insistently defensive tone: 'I call God to witness on my life: it was to spare you that I did not come again to Corinth' (1.23). The emphasis is on motive: 'it was to spare you …' We must assume, therefore, that it was his motives which had been challenged. From the account which follows it is possible to infer reasons for which Paul's failure to come might have been misinterpreted. Was it intended as a rebuke to the Corinthians in consequence of an act of disobedience? Was it a sign of fear that Paul's view might not prevail and his authority would suffer? Was it even (to take our previous argument a step further) the possibility that he would not be able to support himself and would have the humiliation of having to ask the Corinthians for financial help? We cannot be sure. Fortunately, on this occasion, Paul spells out his real motive in some

---

[18]   Derrett art. cit.

detail, and we do not need to be able to reconstruct the criticisms aimed at him in order to follow his argument.

'It was to spare you.' One connotation of this has to be disposed of immediately. To 'spare' someone, you have to be in a position to inflict pain or punishment; you have to have power. What sort of power did Paul have over the Corinthians? Certainly he did have authority – and precisely how this authority was to be exercised in the context of a relationship between Christians is a question that propels the argument again and again in 2 Corinthians. But one thing that it was *not* was that of a 'Lord' (κύριος) over what they believed (their 'faith'). This faith was something of their own, the basis of their new existence (enabling them to 'stand' 1.24). In relation to that, and to the joy it gave them, Paul was better described as one who 'worked with' them rather than as one who 'lorded it' over them. He had made no attempt to use authority to correct belief. The question, as so often in Paul's correspondence,[19] was rather how to act in a particular situation in a way that would be consistent with that belief. It was here that he claimed authority.

What was the particular situation? It was evidently caused by two factors which Paul goes on to refer to: an episode which had caused pain, and a letter which Paul had written to deal with it. It has always been tempting both to identify the episode with something described in 1 Corinthians and to find the 'letter' preserved somewhere in Paul's extant correspondence. But neither attempt has been successful.[20] It seems that neither the issue that caused the trouble nor the letter which it evoked from Paul has left a trace anywhere else. Consequently we have to look only at this paragraph, and at chapter 7.5–12 where Paul comes back to the subject, in order to reconstruct what happened. Since he was writing about something which his correspondents knew all too much about, he had no reason to spell out the details, and all we can do is pick out the outlines. First, there had been pain – pain caused by some individual, that affected the congregation as a whole but was also particularly liable to give offence to Paul (2.5). Paul himself

---

[19] See n. 17.
[20] For an account, see Windisch 9–11.

was absent. He responded with a letter that was written in considerable mental anguish (2.4). It was aimed at showing that the offence was caused as much to the congregation as to himself (2.5): it was for them, therefore, to impose an appropriate penalty. This had been done by the time the present letter was written (2.6). The priority now was to show that Paul felt no further bitterness towards the offender and to ensure that the penalty, once paid, had been followed by the congregation's full forgiveness (2.8), in which Paul himself shared (2.10) – indeed, they could appeal to him for authority to declare it.

Naturally such a letter involved risk – the risk of causing still more offence. Paul himself did not know how it would be received, and in chapter 7 he records vividly the suspense in which he waited to know the outcome. He tells us that it was written to test their 'full obedience' (2.9). That is to say, he must have told the congregation what action they must take; the question was whether they would agree to take it. The issue is hardly likely to have been simply the degree of punishment to which the offender should be subjected, as if the fact of his guilt were already agreed: such a small area of dispute would not have caused the serious pain and tension which Paul describes. It is more probable that the offender had openly challenged Paul's authority on some matter of principle, and forced the congregation to take sides. If so, there will have been a serious danger of their ceasing to look to him for guidance at all, an outcome which would have caused Paul acute anxiety, since it would have called into question the legitimacy of all his apostolic work. His letter, written in the heat of the moment, was clearly intended to bring matters to a head: going along with the rebel would involve abandoning any pretence of devotion to Paul. In the event, but not without further painful scenes, loyalty to Paul prevailed. His letter had been successful as a means of dispelling any illusion that they could simply discard him: 'my aim was to make plain to you ... how truly you are devoted to us' (7.12). The report brought by Titus to Paul, who was anxiously waiting in Macedonia, made it clear that relationships had been fully restored. By the time of the writing of 2 Corinthians, all that remained to be done on the practical level was to make sure that their decision in Paul's favour did not result in an unchristian severity towards the offender (2.7).

'Thanks be to God' (2.14). Any recollection of success or good fortune was enough, in Paul as in other Jewish writers, to trigger off a brief exclamation of thanksgiving, and that may be sufficient explanation of the little hymn of praise that rounds off the section. But it is also possible to trace a closer connection with what has gone before – and in any case it would not have been like Paul to allow his argument to rest at a purely human level: there was, as so often, a Christian meaning to be extracted from it. Two metaphors are employed in quick succession. First, Paul is like a captive in a triumphal procession,[21] being led forward by God in the cause of Christ – his apparent success, that is to say, is as little his own as is the victory that of a prisoner of war. Secondly, the efficacy of his work for Christ may be compared with a scent, a fragrance, which is also a catalyst, a means of discrimination between good and bad. Ancient biology was familiar with the observation that what pleases the nostrils of human beings may be deadly to certain animals. Aristotle had noticed that vultures can be killed by perfume,[22] just as small birds can be affected by the smell of polish or embalming. Here, then, was a metaphor for one of the great mysteries of religion. It was easy to say – it was common currency in religious language, with its roots in sacrificial rituals – that good words and actions offer a 'sweet savour' to God.[23] Why, then, does not everyone find them attractive? Why do some actually react so violently against them that they cause their own downfall? It seems to belong to the presence and activity of God in the world that it can be a cause, not just of life to those who believe, but of death to those who, through human wilfulness and sin, persist in rejecting the message and the example.[24] Paul, involved in this same mysteriously

---

[21] Attempts to remove the connotation of a *triumphal* procession in θριαμβεύω cannot be justified. Cf. *HNT* 198, where Kümmel corrects Lietzmann (108). Scott J. Hafemann, *Suffering and Ministry in the Spirit* (USA: Grand Rapids 1990) 19–34, shows that θριαμβεύοντι ἡμᾶς must mean 'leading me as a captive' and adduces evidence that such captives were normally killed.

[22] *de mirab. auscult.* 147 (845a). Other references in Windisch 98.

[23] Gen. 8.21 etc.

[24] Cf. T. W. Manson, '2 Cor. 2.14–17: Suggestions towards an exegesis', *Studia Paulina* (F S de Zwaan), Haarlem 1953, 155–62, who assembles the evidence noted by Wettstein and S.-B. for the rabbinic assumption that the Torah could be both elixir and poison. Note also the double meaning of φάρμακον = medicine *or* poison e.g. Ign. *Trall.* 6.2, *Eph.* 20.2.

double-edged agency of God, must expect similarly dramatic consequences. Had his letter been rejected, this is how he would have had to see it: the truth causing destruction to those who resisted it. But, in the event – thanks be to God!

But to use this metaphor, of the 'fume and fragrance' of Christ, with regard to the activity of any human being is to make a crucial assumption: that everything the person says and does is entirely motivated by God. If people react adversely to the message, may it not be because of the personal bias of the messenger? If people do not accept the testimony, may it not be because of the dubious character of the witness? To speak of oneself in terms of being an agent of God for life or death, a kind of litmus paper to distinguish between good and evil, is to make an enormous claim – that one's motives are perfectly clear, that one is totally transparent to the purposes of God. 'Who is equal to such a calling?' (2.16). In principle, the answer must be 'no one'. But one can at least make a start by eliminating possible sources of misunderstanding and suspicion. The notion of a teacher of philosophical or religious truth making his living out of it, and therefore being able to adapt his teaching to what people wanted to hear, had been criticized from Plato[25] onwards, and Paul uses here a word (καπηλεύειν) that was a standard weapon in the argument: '*trafficking* in the word of God'.[26] Fellow apostles were more vulnerable to this criticism than he was, since they took advantage of the right (which Paul conceded to them) to be paid for their work. But Paul himself, by deliberate choice, had never done so. On these grounds at least, he could claim absolute sincerity: an adverse reaction to him was that much more likely to amount to a rejection of the very word of God.

We now encounter one of the great difficulties which confront the interpreter of Paul. Paul asks (3.1) if he is beginning to 'commend himself' again, and refers to letters of commendation[27] which 'some people' make use of. There are two ways we can take this, and it is not easy to choose between them. One way is to detect, once again, a

---

[25] *Protagoras* 313d.

[26] Philostratus *V.A.* 1.13 (end). There is no warrant for the translation 'diluting', cf. Hafemann, op. cit. (n. 20) 101–114 except in so far as any form of 'trafficking' creates the temptation to dilute the commodity for profit. Cf the discussion in Thrall, 210–15.

[27] Full references in Lietzmann *HNT* 110.

defensive note in Paul's voice: people must be criticizing him for spending too much time trying to 'commend himself'; in reply to which he contrasts himself with those who believe that 'letters of commendation' are necessary for one who claims to be an apostle, and retaliates by pointing out how absurd such an idea would be in his own case. If this is correct, it gives us a precious insight into the character of the opposition Paul had to contend with in Corinth: people who were challenging Paul's authority on technical grounds and pointing to their own superior credentials. Certainly this is not the only time that we glimpse such opponents in this letter: the question of the qualifications needed to be an apostle is raised several times, and Paul seems to have to defend himself against an attack on these lines. But whether 'letters of commendation' came into the dispute is perhaps not quite so obvious; for there is a second, quite distinct, way in which the present passage may be approached. Paul is about to develop an idea worthy of the English Metaphysical poets: that real 'letters of commendation' are written, not on paper, but on human hearts – his friends *are* his commendation. And this leads to a further thought. 'Writing in the heart' recalls another contrast: Moses wrote on stone tablets, but there was a prophecy of Jeremiah (31.33) that there would be a new covenant written on the 'tablets of the human heart' – and this in turn leads to a discussion of the finite, provisional character of the Ten Commandments and the greater 'glory' of the new dispensation. At this stage, what we have to consider is this: was Paul stung by his opponents into arguing about 'letters of commendation', and did this lead his mind on to ideas about 'writing in the heart', Moses and 'glory'? Or were these the things he really wanted to talk about in the first place, in which case the 'letters of commendation' may simply have been a rhetorical motif, a convenient way of introducing a new topic? There is no way of answering this question with any certainty; and we must beware of building up an elaborate profile of Paul's alleged opponents on the assumption that only the first answer is correct.

In any case, before Paul proceeds to the larger point he has in mind with regard to Moses and 'glory', there is further mileage to be had from the Jeremiah passage, this time in the direction of his own work and authority. If a letter of commendation had been written in the

Corinthians' hearts as a result of his work among them, and if this could be described in terms of the 'new covenant' prophesied by Jeremiah as written on human hearts, then Paul himself could be regarded as an agent in the process of moving people on from laws in stone to spontaneous obedience: he was a 'minister of the new covenant' (3.6) – this was proved by what had now been written in the hearts of his converts as a result of his agency. So here was a further source of the 'confidence' on which he had already laid stress (2.12–15), and also an answer to the question, Who is equal to such a calling? (2.16). No human skills and attributes could provide an adequate qualification; but God could enlist a human being in the task of enabling people to know how to live. He had enlisted Moses to promulgate his laws in written form; he could enlist Paul to promote that new kind of commitment to the cause of God – the 'new covenant' – by means of the activity of the Spirit. And the qualitative difference between conduct regulated by a written law and that inspired by the living Spirit could be expressed in a trenchant aphorism that may also be charged with recollections of Paul's own teaching on law and grace[28] – 'the written law condemns to death, but the Spirit gives life' (3.6).

This parallel, between Moses, the giver of laws to be written on stone, and Paul, the minister of a new commitment to the ways of God inspired in human hearts by the Spirit, has a further implication which takes on enormous significance in the light of Paul's recent near-death experience. What effect did the performance of his task have on Moses? In order to receive the commandments he was to communicate to the people, Moses was obliged to spend forty days and nights in the very presence of God on Mount Sinai (Exodus 34.28). No one with any mystical experience (and Paul certainly had some) would imagine that this could happen to a human being without deeply affecting him; and the writer of the narrative in Exodus makes the point by saying that 'when Moses descended, he did not know that the skin of his face shone because he had been speaking with the Lord' (34.29). The cause of this supernatural radiance in Moses' face would naturally be thought to have been his prolonged exposure to

---

[28] Windisch 111–12 notes also the possible influence of the Greek distinction between human written laws and divinely given 'unwritten laws'.

the unmediated presence of God.[29] But in the world in which Paul received his Jewish education Scripture was interpreted by men whose principal concern was the Law. In those circles it was natural to attribute the change wrought in Moses, not so much to his close encounter with God, as to his first-hand acquaintance with the divinely-given Law:[30] it was this that gave him a radiance such that people hardly dared to look at him. Here, Paul evidently stands in the same tradition. If it was his ministry with regard to the written Law (which incidentally, according to Paul's theology, is a cause of 'death') that gave Moses such radiance, how much greater must be the change produced in one who was a minister of the spiritual law (which, again in Paul's theology, opened the road to justification or righteousness). You could almost say that, in this respect,[31] Moses' radiance was no radiance at all (οὐ δεδόξασται) compared with that of the minister of the new covenant; as we shall see, it was inherently fading and transient (καταργούμενον) (3.10).

In the story in Exodus there is a curious detail: 'Then Moses put a veil over his face' (34.33). The point of this is fairly clear in the narrative. The radiance of Moses' face had dazzled the Israelites; so he placed a veil over it when he came to speak with them. Jewish interpreters appear to have accepted this interpretation: at any rate they rarely seem to have felt that the veil required any comment.[32] But the traditional style of interpretation in which Paul had been educated found hidden meanings in much smaller details than this. It was perfectly normal to look for clues in any features of the narrative that might be thought to be there for a special reason. So with the veil,

---

[29] Philo *Vita Mosis* 2.70 (cf. *Som.* 2.228); Ps. Philo *A.B.* 12.1 seem to assume this.
[30] This becomes explicit in the Midrash, Ex.R 33.1; 47.5 etc. (other references in Linda E. Belleville, *Reflections of Glory, JSNTSS* 52 (Sheffield, 1991) 64 n. 2), but is implicit in the widely-shared reverence for Moses as, above all, a law-giver.
[31] ἐν τούτῳ τῷ μέρει. So Windisch. Some commentators (Héring, Martin) prefer 'partially'.
[32] Belleville, *Reflections in Glory* 69, challenges the statement in S-B (3.516) that there is no Rabbinic comment on the 'veil'. She develops this challenge in 'Tradition or Creation? Paul's Use of the Exodus 34 Tradition in 2 Corinthians 3.7–18', in Craig A. Evans and James A. Sanders, eds., *Paul and the Scriptures of Israel JSNTSS* 83 (Sheffield, 1993) 180–2, citing *Pes.* R.10.6 and Midrash ha Gadol to Ex. 34.33, both of which imply that only the veil made it possible to look at Moses' face (as in Ps. Philo A.B. 12.1). But Belleville still admits it is 'surprising' that there are so few references (181 n. 42).

which is the source of inspiration for most of the rest of the paragraph. Going far beyond what we would regard as a natural or even permissible interpretation of the passage in Exodus, Paul develops the idea that the veil is what actually prevents the true meaning being understood when the 'old covenant' – the Law – is read in the synagogue; and he takes the simple statement about Moses, that whenever he turned towards the Lord (to speak with him) the veil was removed (Exodus 34.34), as a valid description of what happens when anyone 'turns' (i.e. is converted) to the God who is also Spirit[33] and who has given this new 'spiritual' covenant of which Paul is a minister.

But this (as it seems to us) rather contrived application of the idea of a veil is preceded by a striking statement which reads almost like a correction of the biblical narrative. We have seen that the reason for the veil in the Exodus story was that the Israelites were afraid to look at Moses' face. Paul boldly offers a quite different explanation: it was 'so that the sons of Israel should not gaze at the end of what was fading away' (3.13). He has already suggested that the radiance of Moses' face was 'fading away' compared with the new radiance of the Christian minister (3.7). If so, Paul may have asked himself, why was the veil necessary? What needed to be hidden? Was it perhaps his sheer human mortality, the inevitable decay of age, which made it hard for the Israelites to believe that Moses was genuinely an agent of God?[34] Did they find it impossible to believe that Moses' ageing face could communicate the imperishable glory of the Law? In order to

---

[33] An interpretation rejected by Kümmel, *HNT* 200, on apparently inadequate grounds.

[34] The meaning and reference of τὸ καταργούμενον in 3.13 has given rise to much scholarly speculation (see Windisch 120, Collange, *Enigmes*, 94–96). It is complicated by its occurrence in 3.11, where it clearly refers to 'the ministry of judgement' i.e. the giving of the Law through Moses. But the use in v. 13 picks up that in v. 7: 'They could not look at the *face* of Moses because of the glory of his face, which was fading.' Moreover v. 13 follows logically from v. 12: 'We must have great boldness, and not be as Moses who put a veil on his face, so that the sons of Israel should not see …' – see what? Clearly something that Moses had to hide. He could not be hiding the law or its ministry – this was not in his face! He could only be hiding what could be seen on his face, in the first instance the 'glory' (which was fading), then the 'end' of that fading glory, i.e. his own (ageing) face. An interpretation along these lines was suggested by F. Godet, *La seconde épître aux Corinthiens*, (Neuchâtel, 1914) 114 and (I am told) H. A. Kent 'The Glory of Christian Ministry. An analysis of 2 Cor. 2.14 – 4.18', *Grace Theological Journal* 2 (1981) 171–89.

remain credible, did Moses have to conceal his all-too-mortal features behind a veil? By contrast, the confidence of the Christian minister was such[35] that no veil was necessary (3.12): the radiance that attended the communication of the new covenant was in no way affected by the accidents of human frailty.

It is already apparent that this passage will become charged with a rich load of personal meaning if it is brought into relation with Paul's own physical and mental condition at the moment when he wrote it and with his recent near-death experience. But first we must face a question which so far has been simply deferred: the meaning of δόξα, which for convenience I have been translating 'radiance', but which had a wide range of meanings both in secular Greek and in the Septuagint. Why this Greek word was chosen by the LXX translators to represent the Hebrew *kabod* – 'glory' – has never been satisfactorily explained. Certainly there was some overlap of meaning, in that δόξα could mean 'reputation', that is, the esteem in which a man might be held as a result of what he *appeared* to be worth or to have achieved. But in the Greek philosophical tradition, at least since the time of Plato, δόξα had always occupied an inferior position in the hierarchy of values. It meant 'opinion' as opposed to knowledge, a perception that might often be proved false, being based on the appearances of things and not their real nature. Why then was this somewhat ambivalent word used to translate the Hebrew word *kabod*, which in the Bible means nothing less than the 'glory' of God and can describe those moments when human beings catch a fleeting glimpse of the majesty, the terror and the beauty of God?[36] A possible answer lies deep in the psychology of Hebrew religion. God is such that *no human being can ever see him*. If anyone were to do so, the sight would be more than the human senses could endure: 'none can see God and live' – Moses

---

[35] W. C. van Unnik in two articles (*NovT* 6 (1963) 153–69 and *Sparsa Collecta* 2 NovT Supp. 30 (1980) 290–306) has shown that παρρησία describes open, public behaviour 'with uncovered head', as opposed to concealment by darkness and by covering the face.

[36] A history of scholarly discussion of this question may be found in C. C. Newman, *Paul's Glory-Christology* (NovT Suppl. 69, Leiden, 1992) ch. 7. Newman's own solution rests upon establishing a 'semantic field' for δόξα considerably wider than can be supported by the lexicographical evidence.

was always regarded as the one astonishing exception to this general rule.[37] All that could ever be experienced of God was something *like* him, some appearance: a number of Hebrew words had this meaning, of something that was no ordinary human perception but yet fell far short of conveying the ultimate reality of God. One of these was *kabod*, 'glory', which could be used to describe a particularly intense experience of the presence of God, but was also (it has been said) 'a way of safeguarding the appearance of God ... the form in which he chooses to reveal himself'.[38] Other words, such as 'form' or 'shape' or 'likeness', could be used in a similar sense.[39] But 'glory' – *kabod* – was the most vivid and the most comprehensive, and δόξα, with its connotation of some distance from reality, was apparently found to be a reasonable Greek equivalent for it. It was this that the Israelites saw in Moses' face when he descended Mount Sinai. But (Paul has suggested) this was such an imperfect 'likeness' that it was bound to fade even from Moses' features. What was now promised to the Christian minister was of another order: it was permanent (τὸ μένον 3.11).

And so, in the last sentence of the chapter (3.18) Paul can give a precise application to his interpretation of the passage in Exodus. His meaning may best be brought out by means of a commentary:

We all,	*i.e. all Christians, not just Paul*
taking the veil off our face	*as Moses did when he went up Mount Sinai into the presence of God*
see a reflection of the glory of God[40]	*which is as close as we human beings can ever get to his ultimate reality, yet a highly privileged experience*

---

[37] Exod. 33.11.

[38] A. F. Segal, *Paul the Convert* (Yale, 1990) 52.

[39] Ezek. 1.28 etc.

[40] This rendering follows that of the majority of commentators and versions and is paralleled by Philo *Leg. All.* 3.101. κατοπτρισαίμην τὴν σὴν ἰδέαν. But Belleville makes a case for κατοπτρίζεσθαι = reflect, and this seems to be how it was taken by Chrysostom. This certainly gives a better sense: 'we ... reflecting (like a mirror) ... are changed': Belleville, *Reflections of Glory* 278–81, but is barely justifiable as a translation. See Thrall, Excursus iv, 290–95.

and are changed into a veritable likeness of him	*as Moses was, but this time, instead of fading, it progresses*
with ever increasing glory, as was to be expected when the Lord	*the God whose glory we see*
is also the Spirit	*who has made possible this new ministry in the first place.*

The Christian life, that is to say, involves transformation. Through Christ one comes (like Moses) so close to God that one is changed and begins to convey to others something of God's 'likeness' (or glory). But unlike Moses (whose experience was the archetype of ours) the Christian receives this change *permanently*. Nothing can deface it, there is nothing to conceal – an affirmation which may have cost Paul much in terms of courage and faith, given the frightening and humiliating experience of human frailty he had recently endured.

There may be an allusion to this experience in the very next sentence (4.1):

Therefore, having this ministry,	*of conveying God's laws to human beings, like Moses, but writing them spiritually on people's hearts*
inasmuch as we have received mercy	*that is, have been mercifully rescued from imminent death* (1.10)
we do not lose heart.	*(ἐγκακεῖν, a rare word, suggesting fatigue and lassitude,[41] a natural consequence of a spell of physical weakness)*

Paul's critics, as we have seen, would have readily suspected that this near-fatal condition had been caused by unavowed duplicity – things

---

[41] Windisch 132. Thrall, 299, notes that an instance in Polybius supports the meaning 'grow lax', adopted by some commentators.

'hidden for very shame, cunning practices and venal distortions of the word of God' (4.2). But these Paul had decisively 'renounced': the only means by which he would recommend himself was the truth, expressed with a perfectly clear conscience before man and God. Was there, in Paul's case, anything corresponding to the 'veil' that Moses (according to Paul's interpretation) had been forced to put on to conceal his human weakness? If so, it was in the imagination of those who were so utterly in the power of the devil that their minds were 'blinded', they *could* not believe, they were 'lost' (4.3–4). For everyone else, the 'shining' that accompanied a true preaching of the gospel was, again, 'glory' – the glory of Christ, 'who is the likeness of God', that is, a locus in which the reality of God can be experienced by human beings: the 'glory' which may be seen in the faces of those who preach this gospel is a reflection of Christ's glory, a form of service which may be offered to enable others to see Jesus. It was God who created light at the beginning of the world. His creation continues in that supernatural light which now makes it possible to discern the likeness of God in Christ – 'the light which is knowledge of the glory of God in the face of Jesus Christ' (4.6).

Chapter 3

The Renewing Experience

2 Corinthians 4.7 – 7.16

'We have this treasure in earthen vessels' (4.7). This is exactly what has been discovered at Qumran and elsewhere in the Middle East: not only precious manuscripts, but 'treasure' (gold and silver coins), stored in earthenware jars. These jars had a limited function: they could hold their contents together and prevent their dispersal; they could protect them from dust and water. But they could offer no real protection. They could be easily smashed and as easily replaced – indeed, this was one of their advantages: being such ordinary, everyday articles they could disguise the treasure within. Coins could be hidden in one of a row of pottery vessels on the kitchen shelf as effectively as bank notes in the leaves of a book on the bookshelf today. But in themselves they were neither durable nor (unless of superior quality) valuable.[1] If they became contaminated or ritually impure, they were not worth cleansing: they were to be smashed (Lev. 6.28).

Paul has been talking of lasting values – his ministry, the gospel, the light of Christ, the glory of God. He has been talking also of the way in which human beings may be the agents and conveyors of these things – with the danger, always, of attention and reverence being paid to individual persons instead of to the supernatural power at work within them. He now tackles this danger directly. The human agent is as fragile, disposable and essentially unremarkable a bearer of this power as the ordinary household utensil is of a precious object. Were this not so, the powerful influence exercised by Paul and by other Christians on those around them might be attributed to their personal gifts and strength of character. By subjecting even his chosen

---

[1] Barrett, *Commentary* ad loc. prefers to stress this implication of 'earthen'.

agents to the vicissitudes and vulnerability suffered by ordinary people, God has ensured that the power of the gospel should be seen for what it is, and not obscured by the pretensions and accomplishments of its ministers.

How does this work out in practice? If the fact of being entrusted with this 'treasure' gives no immunity from disease, persecution, anxiety or other human afflictions, is the minister simply disposable like a cheap earthenware jar that can be replaced by a visit to the potter down the road? Or does the treasure itself provide inner resources with which to resist the slings and arrows of outrageous fortune? At this point the metaphor of the earthen vessel must be laid aside (though it will come back later): the treasure can do nothing to protect the jar which contains it. But the idea of an inner strength enabling one to cope with outward adversities was a familiar one. In particular, Stoic and Cynic philosophers were keen to demonstrate the power of a truly philosophical temperament to withstand afflictions that would reduce ordinary mortals to anger, resignation or despair.[2] There were of course risks (as we saw in chapter 1) in taking one's own personal experiences as an example: by reciting the particular sufferings to which one had been subjected and which one had borne with stoical fortitude and detachment one might be accused of simply boasting of one's toughness of character.[3] Any such recital must be justified by the circumstances[4] and redound to the credit of philosophy itself, not to that of the individual philosopher. Nevertheless, the example of dedicated philosophers who retained their serenity in the face of severe maltreatment or adversity remained a powerful argument for the truth of the doctrines they professed.[5]

We should not therefore be surprised that Paul's recital of his own afflictions (4.8ff.) – the first of several in this letter – reads like a page from a letter of Seneca or a lecture by Epictetus.[6] The idea was commonplace, and the literary means for expressing it well understood.

---

[2] Seneca *Ep.* 59.8; Marc.Ant. 8.48 etc. For a discussion, see John T. Fitzgerald, *Cracks in an Earthen Vessel* 51–55.

[3] Fitzgerald 107–14.

[4] See above p. 15 n. 38.

[5] Hence the importance of Stoic 'saints' such as Musonius Rufus.

[6] E.g. Seneca *Ep.* 82.14; Epict. *Diss.* 4.7.13–15.

Afflicted, but not defeated – it was the claim of any philosopher who took seriously the power of his convictions to fortify him against adversity. Yet to say that Paul's words have the form of a philosophical apology does not mean that they can be reduced to a piece of conventional self-advertisement. We must examine each phrase in more detail if we are to catch the nuances by which Paul distances himself from the accepted truisms of philosophical discourse.

'At every turn', Paul writes, 'afflicted ... bewildered ... persecuted ... struck down.' Compared with the other recitals of his adversities that come later in the letter, this list is strikingly vague and unspecific; the words seem chosen more for the sake of their opposites ('*not* totally hemmed in ... *not* brought to utter despair ... *not* abandoned ... *not* destroyed') than to describe particular moments in Paul's life. Taken in general terms, they are the *kinds* of vicissitudes which someone might be expected to surmount with the aid of inner resources provided by philosophy or religion: only the references to 'persecution' and to not having been 'abandoned' (presumably by God) seem to make these experiences specific to an apostle. But the picture changes if we assume that Paul was still writing under the impact of the crisis he had recently endured. In 1.8 he described this as an 'affliction' (θλῖψις): here, the very first term in the series of his sufferings is 'afflicted' (θλιβόμενοι). There, his near-death experience made him 'despair of life' (ἐξαπορηθῆναι); here – in the light of his experience of survival as a result of prayer – he speaks of 'near-despair' (bewilderment, ἀπορούμενοι) as opposed to 'utter despair' (ἐξαπορούμενοι, again the word used in 1.8). Whatever the cause of the crisis – personal illness or attacks by adversaries or both – it had involved Paul in 'persecution' from those who saw him as discredited by it and disqualified from preaching a genuine message. And the image of the earthenware jar may make a momentary reappearance when he says he was 'thrown down' but not 'smashed'.[7] Any of these experiences would have been enough to break the spirit of an averagely pious man: Paul sets against them a set of experiences which, in this context, show that something was supplied to him which enabled him to sustain them.

---

[7]   In contrast to Ps 30.13 LXX where the psalmist is like a dead man, a smashed vessel (σκεῦος ἀπολωλός).

What this new resource was he describes with a phrase so suggestive that a number of interpretations is possible:

> at all times bearing in my body the dying and death (νέκρωσις) of Jesus, so that the life of Jesus also should become manifest in my body. (4.10 AT)

The word νέκρωσις is virtually impossible to translate. In the ancient world, the process of dying was felt to begin before the actual moment of death and to continue after it: physical changes could be seen (and smelt!) in the body of a dying person which were thought to be continuous with the progress of putrefaction after death. This whole process, or any part of it, could be called νέκρωσις,[8] which means the condition of a corpse shortly before, as well as after, the moment of death. So what does Paul mean by the νέκρωσις of Jesus? His passion? His death? The condition of his body shortly before, or shortly after, death? Any or all of these may be present in this highly figurative phrase; in addition there may be a hint of a visual image, that of a pall-bearer 'bearing' the actual 'corpse' of Jesus.[9] But the physical associations of the word, which refers not just to the fact of death but to the processes of decay and putrefaction which not only follow it but may precede it as natural harbingers of mortality, point us back to the passage on Moses' 'veil' in the previous chapter. There, as we saw, Paul advanced an unusual explanation for the significance of this veil: it was 'so that the sons of Israel should not gaze at the end of what was fading away' (3.13); and I suggested that what had to be hidden were the physical signs of Moses' mortality, the human message of his ageing face. If this is correct, its relevance would be that whereas the giving of the old Law, though it imparted a certain radiance to its proclaimer, could be rendered ineffective and unattractive by the realities of human mortality, the new gospel imparted a permanent radiance that required no shield from reality: the decay (which might lead to death) of the physical body of the proclaimer in no way dimmed its brightness and

---

[8] See the references cited by Fitzgerald 177–8, to which add Greg.Naz. *Ep.* 152 (MPG 37.257B), where νέκρωσις describes illness.

[9] Suggested by Fitzgerald 178, who notes that Paul uses περιφέροντες which may recall νεκρόφορος.

could be accepted with no attempt at concealment. We may now see, in the striking image of Jesus' νέκρωσις, a significant extension of this idea. Christians bear in their bodies clear signs of their mortality. In Paul's case, this had recently been accentuated by a nearly fatal episode, doubtless leaving him in an enfeebled state. But a Christian is one who (in Paul's phrase) is 'crucified with Christ' (Gal. 2.19). This means sharing that physical decay which precedes as well as follows death. In Jesus' case this νέκρωσις – the complete drama of suffering, death and resurrection – was the means of giving life. In the same way, therefore, the sufferings Paul has just listed, which would normally be seen as a virtual death (and certainly as death to any pretensions to be the bearer of a word of life) could now be seen, certainly not as damaging to the claims of an apostle, and not even to be endured as a test of fortitude and philosophical detachment, but as an aspect (newly discovered through Paul's recent experience) of the Christian's solidarity with Christ. Physical debility and decay, instead of being in apparent contradiction to the promise of life proclaimed in the gospel, are now found to be a means by which the believer identifies with Jesus in his final hours of dying and so makes 'manifest' the new 'life' which was the consequence of that death.

'In the midst of life we are in death.' This popular medieval maxim[10] (perhaps distantly derived from the verse which follows) was doubtless generally understood as a comment on the uncertainty of life in the face of accident, violence and disease. A modern biologist might find a more general sense in it: the process of living itself involves decay leading to death; every living organism, in a sense, starts to die as soon as it starts to live. Paul's next sentence begins with an observation that might be taken as a similar piece of historical or biological realism. 'For we who are alive are constantly being handed over to death.' But it immediately becomes clear why, a few lines later, he concedes that this is a matter, not of observation, but of faith. First, 'constantly' clearly picks up the equivalent word in the previous verse, 'at all times bearing in my body ...'. Secondly, being 'handed over' is a direct reference to the events leading up to Jesus' death: that Jesus was 'handed

---

[10] Ascribed to Notker Balbulus, monk of St Gall in the 9th century. Cf. A. S. Duncan Jones in W. Lowther Clarke, ed., *Liturgy and Worship* (London, 1932) 623.

over' is the most frequent of all statements about his destiny in the New Testament.[11] Thirdly, the sentence continues, '... through Jesus, so that Jesus' life also should be manifest in our mortal flesh'. It is Jesus, in other words, who has made it possible for the vulnerability and decay involved in our mortality to be reinterpreted in the light of his own death and become the means of making apparent the 'life' which he came to impart.

'Consequently death is at work in us, but life in you.' (4.12) As a summing up, this is not quite what we would have expected. The paragraph seemed to have been leading to the conclusion (which is indeed expressed a few verses later) that however much Paul's body (and consequently that of other Christians) might suffer and decay, it would become thereby the vehicle of that true life which was procured for human kind by the suffering and death of Jesus. But now, it is as if Paul dodges away from the suggestion that all he has been through, and the newly positive evaluation of suffering to which it has led him, was all in the interest of himself, so that he, the sufferer (and perhaps others like him), might find meaning in his own tribulations. Suddenly this passage of personal reflection, in which Paul seems to use 'we' as indicating primarily himself but possibly some others in a similar situation, is jerked back into the language of a direct statement to his readers: the beneficiaries of all this are not just me, but *you*. It is as if Paul has suddenly grasped that an experience which he began by recounting in order to silence personal criticisms made against him is of much more universal significance. 'All this', he goes on to say (4.15), 'is for your sake'. The understanding he has gained of the significance of suffering when endured in solidarity with Jesus is a gift, not only, or even primarily, to himself, but to those with whom he can share this new and revolutionary insight.[12]

'For your sake'. The point (that this discovery of a new dimension in suffering was not just a means by which Paul could solve his own problems but a positive gift to all with whom he could share it) is

---

[11] Cf. A. E. Harvey, *Jesus and the Constraints of History* (London, 1982) 23ff.

[12] Cf. M. D. Hooker, 'Interchange and Suffering' in W. Horbury and B. McNeil eds, *Suffering and Martyrdom in the New Testament* (Cambridge, 1981) 71–83 at 78: 'It is because Paul shares in Christ's sufferings that his own are a benefit to others.'

pressed home in another way. The discovery was of course not the result of simple observation, but depended on faith, the faith that the resurrection of Jesus implies the resurrection of believers and their right to be presented in a body before God (4.14). And this seems to have taken Paul back into his meditation (which we detected behind a number of the expressions in this letter[13]) on Psalm 116 (115 LXX). 'I believed, therefore I spoke' – hardly a memorable phrase in itself; but given that it was in Paul's mind along with other phrases from the same group of psalms, it came to hand as a welcome and authoritative endorsement of this link in the argument. The psalmist could be said to have had the same 'spirit of faith' which enabled him to confront his afflictions as Paul had in the efficacy of Christ's resurrection; and this faith had caused him to speak out. In the same way, Paul could say that his own faith-experience was essentially one to be communicated: it was 'all for your sake', and the more people heard of it and gave thanks for it the more God would be glorified.

'No wonder we do not lose heart!' (4.16). The three verses that follow are often regarded as a short summary of what has gone before, making an easy transition to the important new material in chapter 5. But we should be alerted by the emphatic repetition of the rare word ἐγκακεῖν ('lose heart'). In 4.1 it followed Paul's interpretation of his own suffering as a vehicle for the communication of the new and 'glorious' gospel, no longer needing a 'veil' to conceal it from those who, in faith, could understand it to be the very condition which allows entry into the 'life' of the resurrected Jesus; hence they need not 'lose heart'. The repetition of the word here is likely to bring back to mind that whole train of thought, which has just been strengthened and clarified by the argument that the believer's solidarity with Jesus is actually made more intense by exposure to the threat of imminent death. We may detect, once again, an echo of the crisis through which Paul had recently passed, and expect the words that follow to express a decisive rebuttal of those who would regard it as in any way damaging to his credibility. And when we notice that the following five sentences (up to 5.5) all begin with the connecting particle 'for' (γάρ), we are

---

[13] See above, p. 18.

bound to attend to v. 16 as a crucial statement of the conviction to which Paul's experiences of suffering have led him.

We need to translate the sentence literally. 'Therefore we do not lose heart, but even if our outward man is being destroyed, nevertheless our inward man is being renewed day by day.' Note first the double adversative, 'but ... nevertheless' (ἀλλὰ ... ἀλλά): the factor to be set against despair is stated with particular emphasis. Then comes the surprising analysis of the human person in terms of 'outward' and 'inward' – surprising, because this formulation occurs only here in Paul (though the 'inward' half of it occurs in Rom. 7.22), and is not a way in which someone of a Hebrew background would normally have expressed the psychology of a human being. The pair – outward and inward – were of course at home in Hellenistic philosophy;[14] indeed the idea of an inner, invisible and immortal soul inhabiting a transient and observable body was at least as old as Plato. An appropriate scholarly approach to Paul's antithetical phrase is therefore to assume that at this point he dropped into the popular philosophical terminology of the market place in order to describe an experience that was not adequately conveyed by the normal Jewish vocabulary.[15] This may be correct; but we must not oversimplify. The Hebrew culture, like the Greek, was certainly not so naive as to imagine that you could read off everything about a person just by observing looks, gestures, emotions and conduct. Of course there is something going on 'inside' – principally thoughts, feelings, and intentions known only to that individual, or sometimes even unconscious, deep in the recesses of an endlessly devious and often deceitful 'heart'. (Eccles. 7.29) But, more profoundly, there is also a more constant motivation or 'spirit' deep within the visible person, or rather a conflict of motivations: spirit against flesh or sin,[16] or a good spirit against a bad spirit[17] or an external demonic force.[18] The locus of such motivations or struggles

---

[14] See the material collected by Windisch 152–3. The ultimate source is Plato, *Republic* 589a, *Symp.* 216d–e.

[15] So Windisch 153; A. E. Harvey, *Companion to the New Testament* (Oxford and Cambridge, 1970) 582.

[16] Rom. 8.3–4 and elsewhere.

[17] 1 QS 4.23.

[18] Such as the 'unclean spirits' in the synoptic gospels.

is of course out of sight, deep inside: the antithesis between outward and inward is too obvious to require special explanation.[19] Paul gives a classic account of the 'inward' moral struggle in Romans 7, and it cannot be more than an accident that, in that argument, he does not actually place outward and inward together, preferring to speak of 'the inner man' and the (outward) 'limbs' (Romans 7.22f.). If it is true that in the present passage he has made use of a philosophical catch-phrase, this may not be especially significant.

What *is* significant is the verb he uses in relation to this 'inner man': *renewed*. Not only is the Greek word (ἀνακαινοῦσθαι) unparalleled in any literature before Paul,[20] but the idea it conveys goes far beyond what the conventional inward/outward analysis would normally have been used to express. It was one thing for a philosopher to say that the inner man is impervious to outer vicissitudes, or that the immortal soul cannot be harmed by the dissolution of the mortal body; or indeed for the pious Jew to say that adversities may constitute an inner 'testing' by which the character is chastened and purified. It was quite another thing for Paul to say that such experiences actually had a positive value, that they were a source of 'renewal'. Yet it was to this startling conclusion that his previous argument had been tending: acute suffering could be, not only a test of endurance, a tribulation to be borne while awaiting better times, a necessary chastisement and purification of the devout believer (all these approaches to the problem of evil were already on offer), but a means of sharing the mortality (νέκρωσις) of Jesus and so receiving new 'life'. 'Renewal' was an appropriate word for this profound Christian experience.

I have been arguing that this new and unprecedented perception of the positive significance of suffering when it is endured in solidarity with Jesus is likely to have come to Paul through his own near-death experience, and that references to this experience may underlie much of his argumentation in these chapters. We now come to a sentence in

---

[19] Which has not prevented many explanations from being proposed, particularly on the basis of an alleged 'gnostic' dualism. See the survey in R. Jewett, *Paul's Anthropological Terms* (Leiden, 1971) 391–401, and the discussion in U. Heckel, *Kraft in Schwachheit* 256–7, with its rather surprising contention that the 'inner man' means simply 'faith'.

[20] This may of course be an accident; but the early Christian use of the word is certainly distinctive: Rom. 12.2; Titus 3.5; Hermas *Vis.* 3.8, 9.

which the reference becomes explicit. When describing that 'affliction' (θλῖψις), Paul said that 'we were excessively weighed down (καθ᾽ ὑπερβολὴν ... ἐβαρήθημεν), beyond our strength' (1.8). That was how it seemed at the time; but reflection on the experience, on the lines developed in the previous paragraphs, now enables him to use the same words, but in a totally different sense (4.17). The affliction (θλῖψις) which had weighed him down (βαρεῖν) was now seen to be 'temporary' (παραύτικα)[21] and 'light' (ἐλαφρόν): the 'excessive weight' (βάρος), now become still more excessive (καθ᾽ ὑπερβολὴν εἰς ὑπερβολήν), was no longer attached to the affliction but (by a poetic oxymoron) to that which was by definition weightless and (the opposite of 'temporary') 'eternal' – that is, to 'glory'; and from the discussion of Moses' 'glorious' radiance in chapter 3 we know what this means: it is the radiant shining light of the gospel which is such that it is no longer necessary for ageing and decay to be 'veiled'; but it actually shines through and transforms every aspect of our human mortality, using this very fragility as a means of bringing the message of life to others. In short, it is a radical and unprecedented application of a familiar philosophical maxim:[22] lasting reality is to be found, not in transient outward appearances, but in a timeless world behind them (4.18).

All this is sufficiently novel and (in terms of experience) complex to require further elucidation; it would not have been easy for his readers to grasp at once, and the grammatical structure of the following sentences, linked (as we have seen) by the connecting particle 'for', makes us expect that they will offer some more explanation. It is true that this is not the way in which the majority of modern interpreters have taken them.[23] In part, this may be due to the chapter division itself: our modern texts (quite arbitrarily, so far as Paul's original letter-scroll is concerned) make it look as if a new section begins with a new chapter.[24] In addition, certain phrases occur which appear to take their

---

[21] The word, though rare in the Greek Bible, regularly has this meaning in classical Greek; see Windisch 154.

[22] Examples in Windisch 156.

[23] For a survey of opinions, see R. F. Hettlinger, '2 Corinthians 5.1–10', *SJT* 10 (1957) 174–94; F. G. Lang, *2. Korinther 5.1–10 in der neueren Forschung* BGBE 16, Tübingen 1973.

[24] Chapter divisions are said to date from the 13th century.

meaning from reflection on the after-life,[25] and it is tempting to assume that this is the topic to which Paul now turns.[26] The passage is, in any case, extremely difficult and few scholars would claim to have succeeded in interpreting it with complete confidence. My own proposal amounts to no more than following both the grammatical connection of 5.1–4 with what has gone before[27] and the general drift of Paul's argument based (as I have tried to show) on the working out of his near-death experience. Along these lines, an interpretation of this densely-written passage may be offered as follows.

Paul, as we have seen, had recently been faced with the prospect of imminent death. Many of those who had respected his authority as an apostle had now come to doubt his credibility and question his motives in certain practical matters. In this letter, Paul has admitted the severity of his personal crisis, but has protested his total innocence of any attempt to cover up its implications and then gone on to show (in chapters 3 and 4) that the experience itself, far from damaging his credibility, has been a means by which the true 'consolation' and 'glory' of the gospel can be conveyed to others. Instead of causing impotence and debilitation, such an experience, when related to Christ's 'dying', actually causes 'renewal in the inner man'. To explain this startling thought, he has referred back to his discussion of a supernatural radiance or glory, like that which was seen in Moses when he received the divinely-given Law, but now of still greater splendour, such as by its own stupendous 'weight' to make every human affliction seem 'light'. But in this explanation there is still one step to be taken. Paul's experience had not merely been one of extreme 'affliction', of the kind in which the sufferer might be sustained, like the psalmist, by faith in deliverance of God. It had actually made him 'despair of life'; it was a moment of standing on the very brink of death. All that Paul has written about it so far has been from the standpoint of a survivor. It

---

[25] Particular attention is given to the word γυμνός: the Jews 'had a horror of nakedness' etc. But this seems to rest upon M Ber. 3.5, which simply implies that the *shema* must not be recited with no clothes on. A fear of nakedness *after death* is not so easy to document.

[26] The question is then vigorously debated whether Paul had altered his eschatological views since 1 Cor. See the account in Martin, 97–101.

[27] This is also the approach of Frances Young in F. Young and D. F. Ford, *Meaning and Truth in 2 Corinthians* 132–3, though it leads to somewhat different conclusions.

was perhaps not too difficult to see how suffering could be the vehicle of glory – so long as the sufferer was still alive. But suppose it resulted in death: would that invalidate the argument?

Paul has already suggested an answer by speaking of the νέκρωσις of Jesus, a word which covers both the suffering and decay which precede death and the fact of dying itself. But this demands further explanation. How can the physical reality and apparent finality of death be anything but the cessation of every positive feature of the Christian's existence? This question is tackled in the following explanatory sentences.

'For we know ...' That is to say, the answer is not going to be read off the experience itself, but depends on a piece of 'knowledge' which Paul shares with his readers. We are not to expect a private and esoteric thought of his own, but (as it turns out) a doctrine universally held by Christians.

'If our earthly dwelling in this tent is destroyed, we have an eternal dwelling, one not made with hands, in heaven.' Why does Paul describe death as the taking down of a tent? It was not, perhaps, a strikingly original metaphor: philosophers since Plato had used it to contrast the transience of mortal life with the immortality of the soul,[28] and the philosophically-minded author of the Wisdom of Solomon (a book which Paul seems to have meditated upon) similarly wrote of the 'earthly tent which weighs down the inventive mind' (9.15). But the clue comes in the second half of the sentence. A 'tent' was the form which God's 'dwelling' took during Israel's wanderings in the desert. Later, it was given solid form as a 'temple' of masonry in Jerusalem. This was constructed, not arbitrarily, but according to a pattern already existing in heaven.[29] As a building, it was of course impermanent; it had been destroyed and replaced twice since its original foundation. And for Christians it had in any case outlived its usefulness. God's dwelling, for them, was promised to be a building 'not made with hands', that is, the

---

[28] References in Windisch, 158.
[29] An inference from Exodus 25.40 drawn e.g. by Philo *Leg. All.* 3.102.

Christian community itself, the church (Mark 14.58; 1 Cor. 3.16); and this, as the authors of Hebrews and Ephesians saw, was not just the successor of the Jerusalem temple but was the embodiment of that dwelling not made with hands which existed eternally in heaven.[30] This, then, was the Christian's real 'body', of which the believer is already a member but will enter into after death as surely as the earthly 'tent' is replaced by the heavenly form of the 'temple'.

'And here is another part of the explanation' (καὶ γάρ). The fact that we have this expectation after death does not by any means answer the question of how the experience of dying, if it led to death, could be a sign of inner renewal. We need to understand what is happening here and now, in this 'tent' (ἐν τούτῳ).

'We groan ...' This is an unexpected admission. A few verses back, Paul adopted the style (if not the exact phraseology) of the philosopher claiming superiority and indifference to physical and mental afflictions. Is he now, after all, granting that a Christian *is* vulnerable to these things? Or is he saying, 'Yes, we do groan, but our reason for doing so has nothing to do with these afflictions themselves, but is part of our very existence as Christians'? The following words make it clear that it is the second: '... longing to put on over ourselves[31] our dwelling which is from heaven'. We have to ask why Paul seems so ready to make nonsense of his tent/permanent dwelling metaphor: there is no conceivable form of residence which can be 'put on' like a garment. But, just as a temple 'not made with hands' was Christian language for the church, so 'putting on (Christ) like a garment' was Christian language for baptism;[32] and baptism was

---

[30] Heb. 9.11; Eph. 3.10. Thrall, who lists no fewer than nine possible interpretations of οἰκοδομή, rejects this one on the grounds that it does not allow for 'the radical distinction between the believer's present and future existence'. But it is precisely this 'radical distinction' which, in my view, does *not* belong in this context.

[31] As argued by C. F. D. Moule, 'St Paul and Dualism: the Pauline Conception of Resurrection' *NTS* 12 (1965–6) 106–23.

[32] Gal. 3.27; Col. 3.9–10 etc.

the point of entry into the church. For a Christian, the justification for 'groaning' was the consciousness that, though baptized, one had not yet fully 'put on' all that the new life in Christ demanded and made possible, and the constant yearning to put on, as it were, further layers of this covering ...

'... if only we may be found clothed, not naked.'[33] The question has been about death. For a Christian (as for most Jews) death was not just an ending, it was also a beginning; and the first act of the newly-begun drama would be judgement. 'We may be found' – the word refers unmistakably to the moment of appearing before God's tribunal (this becomes explicit in verse 10); and the only possible source of confidence in the light of that judgement will be to have 'put on Christ', first (as a gracious gift) in baptism, then (as a matter of constant yearning and effort) in making one's life conformable with him. Otherwise one will be without a defence of any kind, 'naked'.

'And again, another explanation'. What has just been said is by no means straightforward, and merits being repeated in slightly different words. 'We who are in this tent groan ...', an exact repetition of verse 2, with slight expansion to make clear that it is indeed the 'tent' of a physical body that is being spoken about.

'... in that we do not want, just to take something (the body) off' (which would make us appear naked at the judgement) 'but to put on more and more, so that what is mortal may be swallowed up by life'. Here, at the end of the series of explanations, is a reference back to the crucial statement which the entire sequence (I have suggested) was intended to clarify. 'Mortal ... life': the two words pick up the original sentence which proclaimed the consequence of bearing in one's body the νέκρωσις of Jesus 'in order that the *life* of Jesus may be manifested in our *mortal* flesh' (4.11)

---

[33] ἐνδυσάμενοι, appears to be the older reading, but is rejected in N-A[27] in favour of ἐκδυσάμενοι, a reading which avoids the danger of appearing tautologous. But it is difficult to see why, if it is original, it should have been changed into ἐνδυσάμενοι.

The series of explanations (linked by the particle 'for') is now completed, and before summing the whole matter up Paul adds a new thought. 'Now he that has prepared me for this very thing is God' – a final word to scotch any suggestion that Paul may be taking credit for his stoic endurance: the author of it all is God, who is responsible for all that is beyond normal human capabilities through his Spirit, which is a 'pledge' or 'down payment' (ἀρραβών) for the still richer dimension of existence which is to come. (5.5)

'Therefore ...' The question (I have argued) to which this whole section is addressed is not the speculative one of what happens after death, but the practical and (in Paul's case) highly personal one of whether we can continue to have confidence in the 'life' which is imparted by Jesus, not only in extreme suffering, but actually in death. To which the decisive answer is now given: 'Therefore we *are* confident' (5.6). The immediate reason given for this confidence was the 'dwelling' we have in heaven, something which we can begin to 'put on' (through baptism and subsequent Christian experience) even in this life. The same metaphor of 'dwelling' is now used again. Of course it is true[34] that we must continue to live in our 'earthly tent', or (as it is expressed here) to 'dwell in our body', and to this extent our present existence, or 'dwelling', must be 'apart from the Lord'; for (to use an antithesis which occurs in some such form quite frequently in the New Testament)[35] our day-to-day living can be 'in Christ' only as a matter of faith, not as a visible reality. But we are confident, because death cannot be any kind of disgrace or disqualification; indeed, death is the transition to the condition of solidarity with Christ in the heavenly church-dwelling which is what we are actually yearning and working for all the time, a progressive shifting of our real 'dwelling' from the temporary condition of bodily existence to the eternal security of being 'with the Lord'.

'It follows also ...' (διό, 5.9). The logic here is harder to grasp, because a new factor is introduced at this point of which there has been no hint before, the factor of our *moral* responsibility that will be

---

[34] καί in v. 6 is surely concessive, as in AV, but not in REB.
[35] E.g. 1 Pet. 1.8.

tested before the judgement seat of God. It was of course a matter on which Paul was extremely sensitive, and which he was to discuss in some detail in the letter to the Romans. The more he stressed the gracious act of God in making possible for sinful human beings this life of intimacy with Christ without reference to any moral or religious achievements on their own part, the more he laid himself open to the charge that he was encouraging Christians in the direction of a dangerous (and most un-Jewish) indifference to moral standards. And so here: the more Paul argued (as he does throughout this letter) that physical adversity and even death could be recognized as a positive dimension of Christian experience and therefore carried no imputation whatever of moral failure and delinquency, the more he laid himself open to the charge that he was preaching a religion in which right and wrong no longer seemed important: God was being supposed to offer this novel form of salvation to individuals regardless of their moral character. To this Paul had a number of answers: the new life in Christ was such that sinful conduct became almost psychologically impossible;[36] their motivation was now transformed by the Spirit, of which the fruits were always and only good forms of conduct;[37] far from being released from moral constraints, they now lived under an infinitely more demanding code, that of love;[38] and so forth. Here, Paul uses what is perhaps the simplest argument of all. However easily he may have dropped into language which suggests an easy intimacy with Christ, it remains true that what is at stake is nothing less than a human being's relationship with God, and this must always involve the ultimate confrontation between the sinful creature and the perfectly good and just creator – in other words, *judgement*. To put it in conventional terms, 'we must all appear before the judgement seat ...' (5.10). And, as if to emphasize that even the Christian experience of free grace mediated through Christ does not make this a less serious factor in all our thinking, Paul adds that Christ himself, being at the right hand of God, shares God's nature and his necessity to call men and women to account. It is, in a sense, 'the judgement seat of Christ'.

---

[36] Rom. 6.12ff.
[37] Rom. 8.13f.; Gal. 5.22–25.
[38] Rom. 13.8–10.

Given this essential premise to any serious thinking about God, which becomes explicit only at the end of the paragraph, then it makes sense to say, 'It follows that our ambition is always to be acceptable to him'; and it makes no difference what degree of intimacy, of heavenly 'dwelling',[39] we have achieved at the moment of each moral action: our responsibility before God remains as serious as ever. It is at this level – the level of total exposure of all one's thoughts and actions to the judgement of God, rather than of marshalling the arguments and exploiting the rhetorical techniques required to 'persuade human beings'[40] – that Paul hopes to have acquitted himself in the judgement of his readers. And this has a wider purpose than simply to get them on his side: he is not starting another exercise of self-commendation (5.12). The object is to enable them to speak of him, not with shame or embarrassment (given his recent reverses), but with proper pride, and so to have an answer for those who make confident judgements on the basis only of appearances instead of on the reality within.

And now a quite new factor is hesitantly introduced, which has an important influence on the paragraph which follows and which is introduced later on with a similar reluctance. 'If we have been out of our mind, that is a matter between us and God; if we are now speaking rationally and sensibly, we do so for your sake' (5.13). Someone who, like Paul, has had what we would now call a 'mystical' experience will recognize, first, that it is essentially incommunicable to others and may appear totally irrational; it is therefore a private matter, not to be exposed in the public forum of an argument (where only 'rational and sensible' considerations are appropriate); and, secondly, that this makes all experiences or afflictions of the body, or the 'flesh', essentially unimportant compared with the illumination gained from the privileged moments of ecstasy. Certainly Paul's own experience at this

---

[39] Most commentators supply ἐν τῷ σώματι, ἐκ τοῦ σώματος with the two participles in 5.9, which raises difficult questions about moral responsibility and the possibility of sin in an assumed 'intermediate state' between death and judgement. But the previous verses make it equally possible to supply ἐν τῷ κυρίῳ, ἀπὸ τοῦ κυρίου (so Allo: Barrett also allows for the possibility) which makes it simply a matter of how far one has 'put on one's heavenly dwelling' at any particular stage of one's post-baptismal life.

[40] 'Persuading' was widely regarded as the principal object of rhetorical skills, e.g. Quintilian *Inst. Or.* 2.15.3. Paul is repeating more succinctly what he has already said in 4.1–4.

level was such that he had good reasons for not parading it in self-justification. Yet it was an experience which, fundamentally, he believed he shared with all other Christians. He had talked earlier of the experience of being 'transformed'[41] as a result of receiving the new revelation of God's law (3.18); now he speaks of anyone who is 'in Christ' being a 'new creation' (5.17). The effect of Christ's death on behalf of us all (an expression of his love) was that we should all in some sense 'die' (or bear his dying and death, νέκρωσις, in our bodies, 4.10) and begin to live in and for the one who had gone through death for us into resurrection life. Henceforward, therefore, our real 'knowledge' of others will not be in terms of how they appear in 'flesh'. At some stage they – even Paul himself – may have been tempted to think of the crucified Jesus in this way,[42] a source of shame and contempt, foolishness and scandal. But that old, unenlightened judgement has now given way to a new way of seeing things, a new form of existence, made possible by the reconciling activity of God in Christ, a 'ministry of reconciliation' which is now passed on to Christians themselves.

Reconciliation: does Paul's use of this word imply that God was previously estranged from the world, requiring some atonement for human sin before he could establish a relationship with his creatures? So Paul's language, here and elsewhere, has often been taken. But we must beware of pressing metaphorical language about God into logical consequences that it was never intended to have.[43] When, for instance, the Hebrew scriptures speak of Israel having been 'redeemed' by God and brought out of slavery in Egypt, the metaphor well conveys the important perception that it was not their own courageous initiative,

---

[41] The importance of 'transformation' in Jewish mystical experience is well brought out by Alan F. Segal in *Paul the Convert.* See especially 63–71.

[42] A full account of the many possible interpretations of 5.16 is given by Windisch, 186–9; Thrall, 412–20. But we need not be forced by the English phrase, 'knowing someone in the flesh', to assume that Paul means an actual encounter with Jesus during his lifetime. We should be warned against this by the preceding sentence, ἀπὸ τοῦ νῦν οὐδένα οἴδαμεν κατὰ σάρκα, which clearly does not mean 'we never meet anyone' but 'we do not judge anyone by fleshly (worldly, unspiritual) standards'. κατὰ σάρκα should be interpreted along the lines of σαρκικός in 1.12 on which see ch. 2 p. 34.

[43] The unwelcome consequences of doing so may be seen in (for example) the long discussion of this passage in Martin 141–51.

but an action taken by God on their behalf, which had such far-reaching consequences. But there is no suggestion that the redemption price was actually paid to Pharaoh: that would be to press the metaphor into a literal application, for which it was certainly not intended. So here, with reconciliation, we are not to think of two parties each with a case against the other which a skilled negotiator was required to 'reconcile'; that would be to import an unnecessary literalism. Rather we should imagine something along the lines of a Prodigal Son situation. The father maintains his love and yearning for the son, but the son's sin prevents him from believing that he can return to his father. What is required is some agent or go-between,[44] who can persuade the son that his father is not 'reckoning his sins against him' and convince him of the possibility – the reality – of reconciliation. Christ has been such a reconciler. It is now for Christians to take up this urgent message of reconciliation towards others: the sin of us prodigals has been so fully accepted and dealt with by the reconciler that, through him, we can now return to the father with nothing against us left in our record. We have – Paul can even strengthen it by saying we *are* – the righteousness of God as a result of our association with Christ.

'Working together (with God) …' (6.1). A Jewish, and even a Christian, theologian might doubt whether this is an acceptable idea:[45] it is surely almost blasphemous to suggest that a human being could actually stand alongside God and 'work with him'. But this is to ignore the immediately preceding train of thought. God sent an agent into the world to bring about reconciliation. That agent (Christ) now has further agents ('ambassadors') who encourage and promote this reconciliation in others. It is all God's 'work', and the agency, which may be called 'representation' or 'ministry', takes the form of an urgent appeal (once again: παρακαλεῖν). Paul evidently feels that this appeal must still be addressed to his Christian readers. He has begged them

---

[44] I have explored this concept against the background of Jewish 'agency' in 'Christ as Agent' L. D. Hurst, and N. T. Wright, eds, *The Glory of Christ in the New Testament* (G. B. Caird FS) (Oxford, 1987) 239–50.

[45] Philo *Quod Deus imm. sit* 87; *de Som.* 1.158; Chrys. ad loc. (BP p. 136), οὐδένος γὰρ ἐκεῖνος δεῖται. 'God' is of course not the only complement that can be supplied to συνεργοῦντες, but is assumed by the great majority of commentators.

'on behalf of (i.e. as an agent of) Christ' to be reconciled to God; now he urges them not to receive God's grace 'in vain'. What this means, and why the Christians in Corinth should be running such a risk, is not clarified by the text he quotes from Isaiah: this (as in the case attributed to Jesus in Luke 4.19ff.) appears to be simply a preacher's gambit for stressing the urgency of the appeal. What lies behind this sudden admonition has to be inferred from what follows: 'giving no offence in anything, so that the ministry is not brought into disrepute' (6.3). With these words Paul returns to what has been a guiding theme of the letter. His personal reverses, and certain decisions he has taken and styles of conduct he has adopted, have appeared to do precisely this – to cause offence and to bring the ministry into disrepute; and it would follow, of course, that if the messenger was discredited the message too would lose credibility.[46] He has shown how each of these inferences has been false, and in particular how his near-death, far from calling his message into question, is actually a means of mutual encouragement and of deepening the Christian understanding of suffering. He is, to this extent, like a Stoic philosopher who can properly 'commend himself' as a 'minister' of the true path through life by listing the afflictions and trials through which he has passed and the inner resources which have enabled him to 'endure' them. And so, still in the style of a defender of philosophy,[47] he embarks on a recital of his vicissitudes and of his resources for enduring them (6.4–10). This time (compared with the previous list in 4.8–9) he is a little more specific: 'beatings' and 'imprisonments' are known items in his biography,[48] 'labours, sleepless nights and fasting' seem to be self-imposed hardships, due perhaps to his determination to support himself financially and not be a 'burden' to his churches,[49] 'holy spirit' and 'love without deception' are cardinal features of his portrait of the Christian life.[50] The recital ends with a series of paradoxes, which

---

[46] Cf. Fitzgerald, *Cracks* ... 188–90 who puts the matter in the context of a well-known philosophical debate: should one care about public opinion?

[47] See the material assembled in Fitzgerald, *Cracks* ... ch. 3.

[48] 2 Cor. 11.23; Acts 16.23; etc.

[49] Cf. R. F. Hock, *The Social Context of Paul's Ministry* ch. 4.

[50] Gal. 5.25; Rom. 12.9 etc.

again would recall the claims of Cynic philosophers to 'make others rich by their poverty' and so forth.[51] But our attention is caught by the reappearance, in the midst of this philosophical-sounding language, of phrases from the psalm which, as we have seen, was much in Paul's mind when he wrote this letter:

> I shall not die; I shall live
> to proclaim what the Lord has done.
> The Lord did indeed chasten me,
> but he did not surrender me to death. (Psalm 118.17–18)

These words, certainly, express a spirit of endurance similar to that of the philosopher; but they are also a reminder that the source of it is, not philosophy, but God. And when Paul offers a vivid rewriting of the psalmist's 'I shall not die but live' –

> 'as dying, and behold we live' (6.9)

– it is difficult to resist the conclusion that he is referring back, once again, to the moment when he 'despaired even of remaining alive'.

'I opened my mouth and drew in my breath'; 'you widened my heart'. These phrases from Psalm 119 (LXX 118.32), expressing a longing for, and a readiness to respond to, God's commandments, seem to have given shape to Paul's feelings as he turns directly to the Corinthians and tells them that, far from being offended and constrained, he is, as always, affectionate and open. The constraint, if any, is on their side; they owe him a comparable openness in return.

(The short passage which follows (6.14 – 7.1) interrupts the argument. This much is agreed by scholars; but they agree on little else.[52] The diversion from the main line of thought, the number of

---

[51] See Fitzgerald, *Cracks* ... 195–201 on the philosophical background to all these antitheses.
[52] The various positions, and the weaknesses of each, are well summarized by Martin 190–95, who argues that Paul edited and inserted some pre-existent material, and Thrall 25–36, who argues for Pauline authorship; see also H. D. Betz, '2 Cor. 6.14 – 7.1: An Anti-Pauline Fragment?' *JBL* 92 (1973) 88–108.

words and expressions unexampled in Paul, the similarity of thought to that found at Qumran, and above all the apparently un-Pauline sectarianism, aiming at creating a pure and exclusive community – all these add up to a formidable case against Paul having been the author. Yet all these points are capable of being answered: there are other instances of Paul introducing a parenthesis or digression and then returning to his main point; his vocabulary is strikingly original in other passages; he may well have shared some 'Essene' ideas without actually having to borrow them; and the apparent exclusiveness he was recommending may have been no more than a particular emphasis, required by the circumstances, or by that need for clear standards and boundaries which will be encountered at some stage by every Christian community. These counter-arguments certainly do not carry the day; but at least they make it possible to avoid having to answer the most intractable question of all, namely, why anyone other than Paul should have placed such an uncouth insertion in a passage that runs smoothly without it. As for an 'accidental' displacement: scrolls of papyrus could not have a piece inserted in the way that an extra leaf might find its way into a book; and the passage hardly reads like a gloss or a comment which someone might have written in the margin and which a scribe incorporated in the text of a subsequent copy.[53] The matter remains mysterious and is probably insoluble. I have nothing to add to the debate myself; and since it is widely agreed that the passage is not germane to the main argument of the letter, I propose to leave it out of account, though leaving open the question whether it comes from Paul himself.)

The appeal for openness continues in 7.2; but this time Paul seems to revert immediately to self-defence: 'I have not wronged anyone, I have not ruined anyone, I have not profited from anyone.' These words confront us with a problem we have met before. They could refer to actual charges which had been made against Paul, and which he still

---

[53] This is the way 'interpolations' normally came about. So far as we know no scribe ever did anything but copy what he thought ought to be in the text; but he might not distinguish between a reader's (or editor's) *comments* and *corrections*: both would have been written in the margin.

felt the need to rebut. In particular we could see in the word 'exploit' (πλεονεκτεῖν) a reference to accusations of dishonesty in managing the collection of money which Paul was to confront explicitly in 12.17–18. But equally these words could be drawn from the standard repertory of phrases used by a righteous man to protest his innocence in the face of those who drew a damaging inference from his afflictions – similar expressions can be found in the psalms and in Wisdom literature (which were demonstrably at the back of Paul's mind), and if indeed Paul had recently survived a particularly life-threatening experience they would be an appropriate way of reiterating his innocence and the 'assurance' (παρρησία)[54] with which 'the just man … confronts those who oppressed him' (Wisdom 5.1).

Either way – whether the words are specific or conventional – Paul is defending himself; and in a Jewish court any form of self-defence could have practical consequences.[55] A successful defence might become an effective prosecution: by proving one's innocence one would be directing the judge's attention to the offence of the plaintiffs in bringing the accusation in the first place. Taken in this way, Paul's words might have been uncomfortable for his readers, and he hastens to reassure them, giving characteristic theological depth to a conventional expression (7.3). Any friend might say to another, I am with you for life or for death, for death and for life.[56] In themselves, Paul's words (which repeat an assurance he has given before) could mean no more than this; but now they are also a reminder of the deep perception he has expressed earlier of the significance of death in imparting new life (4.12). It is this which is his ultimate source of encouragement (παράκλησις), and which enables him to say without affectation that even the afflictions he has recently endured have brought him 'joy' (7.4).

One of the themes of this letter, which dominates its first paragraph, is the mutual 'encouragement' which Christians may give one another

---

[54] AV's 'boldness of speech' comes closer to the meaning of παρρησία than modern renderings such as 'confidence in you' (RSV, JB) 'I boast about you' (NRSV), 'great frankness' (REB). On the word, see above p. 51 n. 35.

[55] On this see A. E. Harvey, *Jesus on Trial* (London, 1976) 110.

[56] References in Bultmann 179f. There is no significance in 'death' coming before 'life', cf. Euripides, *Orestes* 307f.

even in the midst of their sufferings – one of the meanings of the versatile word παράκλησις, which applies, Paul reminds us, to relationships not just between ourselves, but also between ourselves and God – God who 'encourages the humble' (7.6 – an allusion to Isaiah 49.13). Here, the theme is illustrated by the sequel to the episode which Paul began to narrate in chapter 2. He had written to the Corinthians a letter which cost him many tears and could well have caused them hurt (though this was not his intention, 2.4); he had been in such suspense over the outcome that he had to abandon his work in Troas and wait for news in Macedonia (2.12–13); to his great relief, he had learnt that all was well – but this part of the story had been passed over very rapidly, and Paul returns to it here, with an explanation of how the news of their reception of that severe letter could mean, not just personal relief to him, but an equal encouragement to Titus (who had first received it and then conveyed it to Paul) and a cause for the deepening of their relationship through the experience of hurt turning to repentance, reparation and renewed mutual respect and affection. The result was that Paul could now speak of his delighted 'confidence' in the Corinthians (7.16). Sometimes, doubtless, this was no more than a manner of speaking: then as now, letter-writers would tell their correspondents that they 'trusted' they would do such and such, that they had 'confidence' in their willingness to help, and so forth.[57] It was a familiar way of pressing a case or asking a favour – a device Paul uses at the beginning of chapter 9. But here there is nothing formal or contrived. Paul is undoubtedly recalling the 'encouragement', the assurance and the sense of complete mutual confidence which this delicate episode had engendered. His language is warm and heartfelt; and it throws into relief the sense of shock and uncertainty which had been subsequently caused (if we are right in this supposition) by the Corinthians' adverse reaction to Paul's near-death experience. The fact that a 'God-oriented' way of receiving a hurt had led to such an enrichment of their relationship would have

---

[57] Cf. S. N. Olson, 'Pauline Expressions of Confidence in his Addressees' *CBQ* 47 (1985) 282–95: 295, 'The epistolary expression of confidence is best interpreted as a persuasive technique rather than as a sincere reflection of the way the writer thinks the addressees will respond to his proposals or to himself.'

made it all the more devastating that a 'flesh-oriented' reaction to his physical condition had led to distrust and estrangement. It may indeed be the disturbing contrast between the consequences of these two episodes, and the need to recall the first as an antidote to the second, which account for the alternation of moods in this letter: here, a warmth and serenity virtually without parallel in Paul's letters – only Philippians comes anywhere near it; elsewhere, a tension and a sensitivity to misunderstanding which caused Karl Barth to call 2 Corinthians 'that long-drawn-out, harassed groan'.[58]

[58]   *The Epistle to the Romans* (E. T. Oxford, 1933) 258.

Chapter 4

The Commissioning

2 Corinthians 8–9

At this point modern scholarship places us before another difficult choice.[1] The two chapters that follow can each be read as an entity in itself. There is no obvious connection with what has gone before: the subject switches abruptly to the arrangements for the collection and to Titus' part in it. Suppose therefore that they originally existed independently: what would they have been written for? There are clues in the language, which contains a number of technical terms belonging to the world of administration, a world in which 'letters of recommendation' played a significant role. Moreover, Paul seems particularly anxious to persuade his readers to adopt a particular course of action in which Titus is to play a significant part, and uses a number of ploys that are familiar from standard textbooks of ancient rhetoric and would have been among the resources that any civil servant might have used to get a bit of business done at a distance, writing a letter of recommendation which not only introduced the intermediary or agent but also prepared his recipients for whatever he would be asking them to do. May we therefore have the actual 'letter of recommendation' here which Paul wrote to recommend Titus to the Corinthians – or rather two such letters, since chapter 9 seems to start all over again with no reference to the 'commendation' which has just been given in chapter 8? All we would then have to imagine is that some early editor, anxious to include these letters somewhere, simply removed the opening greetings and concluding farewells and inserted them at a

---

[1] For a full account of the history of NT Scholarship in relation to 2 Cor. 8 and 9, see H. D. Betz *2 Corinthians 8 and 9* (Hermeneia) (Philadelphia, 1985) 3–35.

point in '2 Corinthians' where they did not disturb the flow of any argument.[2]

This explanation is plausible and we shall look at some of the evidence for it as we go along. But, even given the presence of clues which point invitingly in this direction, there is an alternative which we have to keep open. This is that this section follows on from the preceding one,[3] and that Paul begins to write *in the style* of a commendatory letter, making use of civil-service-type language in order to avoid the embarrassment of having to speak explicitly about sums of money and arrangements for their safe conveyance – an embarrassment to which he seems to have been particularly sensitive and which forced him to use similarly oblique language elsewhere.[4] Paul certainly had an urgent request to make of the Corinthians, but of the kind which he always preferred to speak of somewhat indirectly. He also evidently needed to express his personal confidence in Titus, who would be assisting in the transaction. What more natural than that he should adopt a more official tone and use some well-tried techniques of persuasion?

There is no way of deciding with certainty between these alternatives. But if there are threads in these chapters which can be found in the texture of earlier chapters, this would be a reason for inclining towards the second view. And in fact the very beginning of chapter 8 shows a remarkable affinity to the sentence which occupied our attention so much right at the beginning:

> We should like you to know, my friends, how serious was the trouble (θλῖψις) that came upon us ... (1.8)

> We must tell you, friends, about the grace of God given to the churches in Macedonia. The troubles (θλίψεις) they have been through have tried them hard ... (8.1)

---

[2] For a substantiation of this view, see Betz, *passim* and especially the discussion of method 129–40.

[3] As is still the view of a number of commentators e.g. P. E. Hughes, *Paul's Second Epistle to the Corinthians* (London, 1962) xxi.

[4] A notable example is Philippians 4.10–19, which discusses a vexed question of finance without once mentioning money!

It is not suggested that the churches' 'troubles' were comparable with Paul's nearly fatal experience; but much of the letter so far has been occupied with explaining how such 'trouble' could in fact issue in 'life' and 'encouragement'. Similarly, the troubles of the Macedonians have resulted in their being 'exuberantly happy' – the same pattern is repeated, even if in a less dramatic scenario. It cannot be said that chapter 8 introduces a totally new theme.

But here the same pattern is the frame to a new thought. As affliction leads to exuberant joy, so abject poverty leads to exuberant wealth. The language is of course figurative to a certain extent. The poverty spoken of here is not utter penury, the wealth is not material riches – the parallel drawn with Christ a few verses later makes this clear. The Macedonians may certainly have been relatively poor – poorer, in any case, than the Corinthians, given that Macedonia was distinctly less prosperous than Corinth;[5] and the phrase, 'the wealth of their liberality', implies[6] simplicity in their way of life, austerity in their provision for their own needs and perhaps a willingness to make personal sacrifices, resulting in an abundance of the 'wealth' which is expressed in open-handed generosity from the base of a consistently simple life-style.

The extent of this generosity is expressed with what may reasonably be called rhetorical fulsomeness. The Macedonians made their contribution

- beyond their powers
- spontaneously without pressure from Paul
- begging to do so with much urgency
- beyond Paul's expectations
- giving their very selves. (8.3–5)

Characteristically, Paul does not mention the amount they gave, or indeed that he is talking about money at all. He calls it a 'favour' and a 'partnership in this service towards a Christian community'. The

---

[5] Betz 50–51.

[6] ἁπλότης is used to denote a generosity born of simplicity and sincerity rather than wealth and ostentation: AG s.v., Betz 44–5.

words have an official sound:[7] as used by an administrator they would cover anything from formal patronage of a worthy cause to direct financial support; they would denote the contribution the Macedonians had made without being embarrassingly specific about exactly what they had given. But they were also words which, in Paul's vocabulary, carried a rich load of Christian meaning. 'Favour' (χάρις) is also 'grace', which describes the God-given character of the Macedonians' whole response. It describes also the way in which Christ turned his deliberate 'poverty' into wealth for others (8.9). 'Partnership' (κοινωνία) is also that distinctive solidarity within the community which binds Christians one to another, and which would be deepened and strengthened by the Macedonians' act of generosity towards their fellow-Christians in Jerusalem. 'Service' (διακονία) is infinitely more than an administrative act of submission: it is the fundamental quality of relationships within the Christian community.[8] The language, we may agree, is such as might have come naturally to a civil servant in the Roman Empire; the rhetoric likewise. In Paul's hands it resonates with theological overtones.

The point of dwelling on the example of the Macedonians was of course to shame the Corinthians – a familiar rhetorical device technically known as 'comparison',[9] bringing with it a touch of hyperbole ('you are overflowing in every way, in faith, in speech, in knowledge and all zeal') which, however sincerely meant, is clearly intended to reinforce the appeal to their generosity. Indeed, lest it be read as a list of formal compliments, Paul includes his own love for them which is to be reckoned among *their* spiritual riches. Mixed in with the rhetoric, again, are some terms that belong to the vocabulary of administration.[10] The result of the success of the collection in Macedonia had been that Paul 'commissioned' Titus to 'complete' the same task in Corinth – but lest this should sound like an official 'order'

---

[7] See Betz 46 for the evidence for technical uses of χάρις ('favour'), κοινωνία ('partnership') and διακονία ('public service').

[8] See the study by J. Collins, *Diakonia* (New York, OUP, 1991).

[9] For a study of σύγκρισις in relation to Paul, see C. Forbes, 'Comparison, Self-praise and Irony: Paul's boasting and the Conventions of Hellenistic Rhetoric' *NTS* 32 (1986) 1–30.

[10] παρακαλεῖν = 'summon' or 'appoint', O Schmitz, *TWNT* 5.772–3 (A1); LSJ *s.v.* II2; ἐπιτελεῖν 'carry out an order', G. Delling, *TWNT* 8.62. More references in Betz 54.

Paul hastens to add that there can be no question of their doing it simply out of obedience: the motivation must be the enthusiastic example of the Macedonians and the sterling quality of their own love. And in any case the project must not be conceived in merely financial or administrative terms: it is a 'favour' (8.6) which implies something given without any obligation and which makes possible a comparison between this act of generosity and the gracious self-giving of Jesus: their material gift may be a means of enriching others spiritually, just as they themselves have been enriched by Jesus' self-impoverishment.

Paul may not be giving an 'order' but he has a very definite view (γνώμη)[11] on the matter: it is 'in their interest' to complete their contribution. From this they might have thought he was going to suggest a practical reason; but the 'interest' is a very much more subtle one. Ancient moralists laid great stress on the importance of *intention*, whether in criminal acts (an unwitting offence was less serious[12]) or in acts of charity (a deed is good only if it results from good intention[13]). When, in the previous year, the Corinthians had first started on the collection, they had not treated it like a tax or an imposition: they had 'wanted' to do it, it was genuine charity. In which case it would be discreditable to them if they now failed to carry out their good intention: it was 'in their interest' to do so. Furthermore, since their intention mattered as much as the actual giving, there was no excuse for saying that they could not afford to keep their promise; their intention would be fulfilled, and their gift would be entirely acceptable, as a proportion of their actual means, not in relation to an assessment of what in other circumstances they might have been able to pay. Paul's appeal, that is to say, is becoming increasingly pragmatic, we might even say worldly. He began with the example of the Macedonians, who had gone through a considerable amount of affliction (θλῖψις) in order to create abundance for others. He might have used this example to exhort the Corinthians to accept a comparable degree of hardship for the sake of the Jerusalem church.

---

[11] A *sententia*. For the rhetorical use of this, see Betz 63.
[12] Num. 15.27–31; Aristotle *Rhet.* 1.13. 1373b; Ps. Phok. 51–2.
[13] Seneca *Ep.* 95.57.

But in fact the line he follows is quite different – we might even say it is worldly, non-Christian. Greek lawyers and philosophers laid great stress on the importance of 'equality'.[14] Society is stable and harmonious only to the extent that the citizens have equal rights and benefits. The idea was strange to the Jewish culture; but it was possible to find it in the Bible by implication, and Paul was not the only Jewish writer known to us who saw the distribution of the manna in the desert ('to each according to his need') as an example of the 'equality' inherent in God's justice.[15] Thus, to round off his appeal, Paul underlines its sheer reasonableness: the Corinthians are not being asked to do more than make an adjustment of their own wealth relative to that of their fellow Christians in Jerusalem. The same principle would apply (in reverse) if Jerusalem were better off than Corinth. Natural justice – which is also God's justice – demands that there should be an interchange to create 'equality'.

We have already heard that Paul had 'commissioned' Titus to complete the administration of the collection in Corinth. From a formal point of view, it only remained to record that Titus had accepted the commission (8.17),[16] and since the Corinthians already knew Titus no further commendation might have seemed necessary. But Paul has more to say about him. Any official should be expected to show 'zeal' in carrying out his appointed task; the quality was the first one looked for in any civil servant.[17] But Titus had already shown far more than this in volunteering to go to Corinth: his zeal was not just that of a dutiful subordinate but reflected Paul's own deep concern for the full participation of the Corinthians in the project. At the same time, it was important that the administration should not be in the hands only of Paul's personal delegate. There was the possibility (or perhaps already the reality) of suspicion that the funds might be misappropriated; and conventional wisdom demanded that (as we

---

[14] Philo Q.R.D.H. 141–206 is a treatise περὶ ἰσότητος. Cf. especially 162.

[15] Philo Q.R.D.H. 191 also makes use of Ex. 16.18. Cf. Betz 69–70: 'apparently the tradition was conscious of the ethical implications of the Exodus Haggadah.'

[16] Betz's argument (71) that the παράκλησις of Titus constituted an official *mandatum* seems to go beyond the available evidence. The word here can be given its well-documented meaning (see above n. 10) 'summon'.

[17] Betz 58 n. 141.

would say) justice should not only be done but should be seen to be done – Paul quotes a maxim from Proverbs (3.4 LXX), just as he does in Romans 12.17. So two further independent administrators are commended. The puzzle, for us, is why they are not actually named. It is possible (and many modern commentators have grasped at this explanation[18]) that the names stood in the original letter and were excised in later copies on grounds of subsequent unpopularity or disfavour. But our problem, once again, is to know how far Paul's language is really intended to be official. This paragraph could certainly serve as a formal recommendation to accompany the delegates on their arrival[19] – in which case their names would certainly have been given. Or else Paul could be simply endorsing their official appointment, and adding some personal reasons for receiving them warmly. In this case they would have been known already, and perhaps there was no need to name them. The first, in any case, was widely known among all the churches for his successful proclamation of the gospel, and had moreover been publicly elected for the task (it is interesting to see Paul accepting, and apparently approving of, this democratic procedure in another church). The second is recommended simply on the basis of his long association and collaboration with Paul, in which he has always shown a commendable 'zeal', and is now, like Titus, particularly enthusiastic about the present task. Paul is certainly writing 'on behalf of' all three – of Titus, his personal associate, and the two delegates who are not simply his own agents but are representatives of the churches and whose character and conduct will redound to the glory of Christ;[20] and he ends with a more or less conventional appeal to the Corinthians to demonstrate the love which exists between them to these persons who are not only trusted emissaries of Paul but are official representatives of other churches.

---

[18] E.g. Windisch 262. Barrett 228 assumes that the name (even if not written) would have been mentioned when the letter was read out loud.

[19] Betz 78–82, taking ὑπέρ as indicating 'an act of formal authorization' and citing E. Mayser, *Grammatik der griechischen Papyri*, 1970, 2/2.2 p. 460 (124 AII 5c); but the parallels are not exact. Those under 5b are closer: writing ὑπέρ, 'on behalf of', someone who is ἀγράμματος.

[20] Or 'to the credit of Christ', a use of δόξα known from diplomatic documents, Betz 81–2 nn. 351–3.

Read immediately after chapter 8, the opening of chapter 9 sounds either inappropriate or disingenuous. Paul has just been urging the Corinthians to fulfil their part in the mission of 'aid to God's people' and describing in detail the administrative arrangements he has made. How can he now both say that it is 'superfluous' to write about it and go on to do so all over again? And how, having held up the Macedonians as an example to shame the Corinthians (8.1–5) can he now say that the Corinthians' enthusiasm had been an example to the Macedonians? The sense runs so oddly that those commentators who suppose that originally separate letters have found their way into what we now know as 2 Corinthians[21] are inclined to make sense of the odd beginning of chapter 9 by postulating the beginning of a new letter – possibly, again, one written to provide official authentication for a further group of envoys. The opening would then conform to a stereotype which is as common today as it was in antiquity: 'I am sure I do not need to remind you, but ...'

But this neat solution (for which there is no evidence other than the alleged difficulty of the text as it stands) at once runs into another difficulty. If this is a separate letter of commendation, why should Paul have needed to write a second one to the same addressees, and how are we to explain why he goes over so much of the same ground again? One apparently attractive solution[22] hinges on the word 'Achaia'. This was the province of which Corinth was the capital.[23] We know that Paul worked in other parts of it such as Athens (Acts 17) and Cenchreae (Acts 18.18; Rom. 16.1). Perhaps, therefore, this new letter was not written to Corinth at all, but to other churches in Achaia, who may have got much further with the collection than the Corinthians had, indeed whose record had been so good that they could be held up as an example to others. It is true that Paul usually says 'Corinth' when he is referring to the Corinthians, and occasionally says 'Achaia' when he means, not just the capital, but the whole province (as in 1.1). And the suggestion that at this point he is addressing only the 'provincial' Achaians certainly gets rid of many of our difficulties.

---

[21] For a list of scholars who have developed J. Semler's theory (1776) see Martin, xli–xlii.
[22] Adopted by Windisch 288 and Betz 92.
[23] On Corinth, see J. Wiseman, *ANRW* II 7.1 (1979) 438ff.

But there is one serious objection. It is true that Achaia was certainly the name for the province of which Corinth was the capital; and by adding 'Achaia' to 'Corinth' in his opening greetings Paul was able to include churches other than those in Corinth. But there is no evidence, and little probability, that 'Achaia' could mean the cities of the province *apart from* Corinth, any more than the word 'France' today would be understood as referring to that country *apart from* Paris. And in any case behind any such suggestion lurks a question to which no one can give a satisfactory answer: if chapter 9 was originally a separate letter, why did a subsequent editor include it just here, where it seems to follow so awkwardly on what has just been said in chapter 8?

In view of these difficulties, let me try, once again, to make sense of these chapters as they stand. The problem hinges upon the word 'willingness' (προθυμία) and the statement that Achaia had been 'prepared' since the previous year. How is this to be reconciled with Paul's evident anxiety lest the Corinthians should fail to fulfil their promises and cause shame, both to Paul and themselves, when he came with Macedonian representatives to take delivery of their contribution? Unless Paul had been utterly unscrupulous, and urged the Macedonians to be generous by praising the Corinthians for a generosity they had not shown, it is hard to see how he could ever have used *both* the Macedonians *and* the Corinthians as examples of ready giving. But we must remember that in the previous paragraph (8.10–11) Paul made a point of the Corinthians' initial 'willingness': his concern was that this might turn out not to be matched by their deeds. It is quite possible that this initial enthusiasm was so great that in fact Paul was able to boast of it to the Macedonians (9.2) and so stir the Macedonians to acts of generosity which then exceeded his expectations and allowed him to use *them* as an example with which to stir up the Corinthians when they showed signs of failing to live up to their original protestations. We may certainly think that Paul is being a little fulsome in describing this initial enthusiasm as actual 'preparation' of their contribution; there may be a little rhetorical exaggeration here. But Paul seems almost to concede this when he expresses his anxiety that they may turn out in the event to have been 'unprepared'. The Greek word, after all, can have the same ambiguity as its English equivalent.[24] I may be 'prepared' to join the army when called upon in a national emergency; but that may not mean that I have already got my army boots on. The Corinthians had impressed Paul by the way they had been 'prepared' to help at the outset. It ought to have been, but was regrettably not, 'superfluous' for him to return to the subject now.

In the previous chapter Paul gave an account of his appointment of Titus and two others, of the task they were to perform, and of the response he hoped for from the Corinthians. It cannot be denied that (if this is the same letter) he repeats himself here, referring yet again to this 'commissioning' and pleading that their arrival should not reveal a shameful failure on the Corinthians' part. But here there is also a certain sharpening. We have noticed how Paul carefully avoids mentioning anything so crude as a sum of money; his language, even if it implies a financial transaction, never actually specifies it. He prefers to talk of a 'favour' or a 'service'. He now gives it a still more suggestive name – εὐλογία, literally a 'gift of blessing',[25] understood as a thank-offering made in response to benefits received. It was this kind of gift which they had originally promised. Let not their slowness in completing it provide the pretext for slipping out of it altogether. This might be expected of unwilling tax-payers[26] and parsimonious fellow-citizens, but surely not of the Corinthian Christians!

By way of further arguments that will influence his readers to be prompt and generous, Paul adopts the repertory (as he did in chapter 8) not so much of the Christian preacher as of the conventional moralist. Distinctively Christian conduct is based on love, self-sacrifice and compassion – and Paul has much to say about this elsewhere. But even if this Christian 'wisdom' puts conventional wisdom in the shade, it does not make it obsolete: Paul is always ready to enlist arguments and attitudes that were generally approved of into the service of encouraging good behaviour among Christians. The basis of this secular wisdom was pragmatic and prudential:[27] behave in this way and you

---

[24] See LSJ sv παρασκευάζω B II 3.
[25] Windisch 274, who suggests that there may be a deliberate word play with λόγεια.
[26] Betz 96 n. 57. In Theophrastus *Char.* 22.3 the ἀνελεύθερος is a tax-dodger.
[27] Cf. A. E. Harvey, *Strenuous Commands* (London and Philadelphia, 1990) 145ff.

will be rewarded (in the long run, if not – as so often seemed to be the case – immediately). To promote it down the generations, countless popular proverbs and maxims were coined, memorized and adapted to new situations. In the Bible whole collections were made and endowed with the authority of Solomon, if not of God; but the presupposition behind them – that right conduct pays off in the end – was the same as that of proverbial literature everywhere, and often the maxims themselves were part of an international moral currency. Paul's readers will have been as familiar with it as anyone else, and just as susceptible to its reasonableness as to the more demanding precepts of their new religion.

It is from this common stock of received wisdom that Paul now draws his final arguments. He has three points to make:

(i) 9.6: nature shows that you harvest in proportion to what you sow: the proverb, 'he who sows sparingly, sparingly shall harvest', is reminiscent of Proverbs (11.24) but could equally come from popular country wisdom.[28] Paul applies the converse to reinforce what he has just said: stingy giving will have a stingy reward, giving in the spirit of a thank-offering will bring corresponding 'blessings'.

(ii) 9.7: spontaneous giving from the heart has moral value – again, Proverbs has a maxim that is to the point (22.8 LXX), but Paul may be echoing a widespread maxim[29] with the phrase, 'God loves a cheerful giver'.

(iii) 9.8–10: nature is inherently generous and abundant; so is God; and so you can be. A number of conventional ideas are at work here.[30] In nature, seed is provided, not just for this year's harvest, but for future sowing. 'Sufficiency' is not to be measured by what is just enough for now, but by what 'good work' can be done in the future. God's justice is not a matter of keeping everyone at the level where they happen to be, but provides additional resources for distributing to the

---

[28] Betz 102–5.
[29] Betz 105–8.
[30] Betz 109–16.

poor; so we can afford to use what we have in such a way that it becomes 'thanksgiving' – in the form of thank-offering – to God.

The effect of all this is to encourage the Corinthians, not just to be prompt in meeting the obligation they had originally undertaken, but to do so with generosity. If a cup is half empty, there are two ways of filling it up.[31] One is to 'make up what is lacking', implying that you pour in only so much as is needed. The other way is to 'fill to overflowing' – that is, with the generosity of a thank-offering, which is the way in which all this proverbial wisdom has been tending. And there is more. This 'service' offered to the Christians of Jerusalem is not merely a response to their – perhaps temporary – poverty. Just as, in a Jewish community, Gentile sympathizers would express their solidarity with the synagogue and affirm their obedience to whatever conditions it imposed on them by giving alms to the Jewish poor,[32] so the money that was now to be taken to Jerusalem would rightly be interpreted by the Christians there as a sign of the obedience of Gentile Christians to an ultimate authority in church matters that still lay in Jerusalem and an expression of whole-hearted solidarity with them.[33] As with so many relief operations, its real significance was symbolic: it expressed a depth of relationship between churches of totally different cultural backgrounds for which Paul could only offer amazed thanksgiving to God.

---

[31] See below p. 121.

[32] Klaus Berger, 'Almosen für Israel' *NTS* 23 (1977) 180–204.

[33] Betz 122–5 argues that ὁμολογία refers to an actual document (a usage for which there is evidence in papyrus letters, n. 272) which recorded an agreement of 'submission' (ὑποταγή) by the Gentiles to Jerusalem, and that Paul here reinterprets this as 'submission' to the gospel. The language may be inspired in part by the practice of Gentile contributions to the Temple worship in Jerusalem, on which see HJP 2.309–13.

Chapter 5

The Apologia

2 Corinthians 10–13

Most modern versions and commentaries mark a break at the end of chapter 9; and no wonder. The warmth of feeling which was displayed in chapter 7, and the confident words of recommendation which fill chapters 8 and 9, give place suddenly to a tone of tense self-justification and sometimes bitter reproach. Can this be the same letter at all? What we now know as 1 Corinthians and 2 Corinthians were evidently only a part of Paul's correspondence with the church in Corinth. We have already had to admit some possible disturbance of the text with the intrusive paragraph 6.14–7.1. Is not the tone of chapters 10–13, so different from what has gone before, best explained if this was originally a quite separate letter – either the 'sorrowful letter' alluded to in chapters 2 and 7, or a later letter altogether that may have been provoked by news of further troubles in Paul's absence? Unfortunately there is no evidence of any kind outside Paul's extant letters[1] that can help us, and the few hints he has given us about the situation to which he was writing are quite insufficient for us to be able to reconstruct the sequence of events and then safely fit various sections of the text into it.[2] There is moreover

---

[1] Apart, of course, from Acts. But (a) Acts tends to minimize disagreements of any kind in the church; (b) its narrative follows Paul's movements, and is of no use for reconstructing events in places with which he was merely corresponding. Even where it covers the same ground as Paul's letters, its evidence creates as many problems as it solves. Hence the attempt by John Knox, *Chapters in a life of Paul* (London, 1954) – generally regarded as unsuccessful – to chart Paul's missionary work independently of Acts. A more recent attempt is that of G. Lüdemann, *Paul, Apostle to the Gentiles: Studies in Chronology* (London, 1984).

[2] The quest for the identity of Paul's opponents has been irresistible to many scholars, but no reconstruction holds the field. See especially W. Schmithals, *Gnosticism in Corinth* (E.T. New York, 1971); D. Georgi, *The Opponents of Paul in Second Corinthians* SNTW (E.T. Edinburgh, 1987); D. Oostendorp, *Another Jesus* (Kampen, 1967).

a natural reluctance in the minds of many commentators to break apart what has been handed down to us as a unity unless we are absolutely forced to do so, and it is not impossible to suggest reasons why Paul may have changed his tone at this point. It has been observed,[3] for instance, that the whole of the letter betrays the influence (conscious or unconscious) of the kind of rhetorical training to which Paul is likely to have been exposed at some stage of his life; and since an orator would tend to reserve the more impassioned part of his appeal to the end of his speech, we should perhaps not be surprised if Paul adopted the same strategy in his writing. Or again (as one classic commentary suggested[4]) Paul may simply have had a bad night, and his mood in the morning may have affected the writing or the dictating of the last part of the letter. At the present time no single explanation holds the field. The question why there is an apparent change at this point is best left open. How significant the change is can best be judged when we look more closely at the text.

In the very first paragraph we find features that point both ways – to a continuation of the same letter as much as to a new start. 'I appeal to you' – the word (παρακαλῶ) has been almost a theme-word from the beginning,[5] and just as in chapter 1 this παράκλησις was 'through Christ' (1.5) so here the appeal is made 'through the gentleness and magnanimity[6] of Christ' (10.1). Further on there is a discussion of 'commendation', which seems almost to presuppose Paul's treatment of the theme in earlier chapters (3.1; 4.2; 5.12). But if these are pointers to the unity of the letter, the sudden appearance of specific opponents is an argument for the opposite. Previously, as we have seen, it was always possible to leave the matter open. Paul may have had particular critics in mind; but equally he may have been developing his argument in his own way, conjuring up imaginary opposition and using comparisons that were more rhetorical than real. But now he leaves us

---

[3] F. Young and D. Ford, *Meaning and Truth in 2 Corinthians* (London, 1987) 36–44.

[4] H. Lietzmann, *An die Korinther I.II* (*HNT* 1949) 139: 'I am satisfied with the explanation that Paul had a sleepless night between chapters 9 and 10.'

[5] Even though its root meaning of 'urgent address' can have different applications. Here the context makes it clear that the point is persuasion, not consolation.

[6] The meaning of ἐπιείκεια is well paraphrased by Windisch: undeserved kindness towards enemies and persecutors.

in no doubt: there were 'certain people reckoning that our conduct is according to the flesh' (10.2); and the need to refute their allegations dominates the entire chapter. Whether these criticisms were new, and required a special effort of self-defence, or whether they were the same as those in the earlier part of the letter[7] and now come to the front of Paul's mind as something which he finds he can no longer endure without hitting back more strongly, the singling out of these opponents, and Paul's determination to measure himself against them and to show his superiority to them in all matters of real importance, is by any account a startling change of tactics and style.

What does this accusation of 'conduct according to the flesh' consist of? It is true that, according to Paul's customary analysis of human motivation,[8] the phrase could cover anything from decisions made from worldly considerations to sins of covetousness and self-seeking; yet it may be significant (assuming for a moment the integrity of the whole letter) that the last time 'the flesh' was mentioned was in the context of the 'mortal flesh' which is subject to the decay of death yet is a vehicle for the life of Jesus (4.10–11) – in the context, that is, of Paul's personal testimony that even a near-death experience can deepen our solidarity with Christ and authenticate the message we bear. This testimony was in total contradiction to the usual reaction which people would have to such a crisis when it overtook someone who claimed to be motivated and empowered by God: it would be naturally assumed that his claims to a divinely appointed mission were false and that his motives could no longer be trusted. Such reactions would come to a head when the sufferer actually made an appearance: he would bear the humiliating marks of the condition from which he was only just beginning to recover, his activities would be limited by the weakness of his 'flesh', and he would have lost the ability to do that by which he had always set particular store, namely to support himself during his visits and to lay no burden of care and hospitality upon his hosts.

'Certain people', in any case, were making attacks on him of this kind; and Paul is equally specific about one of their criticisms, to

---

7   E.g. the charge of making decisions 'according to the flesh' in 1.17 or the suspicions
      which appear to have gathered round the arrangements for the collection, 8.20.
8   Rom. 8.1–13; Gal. 5.19–21.

which he has already alluded in verse 1, and which he now repeats verbatim: 'his letters are weighty and powerful, but his bodily presence is weak and his speaking is contemptible' (10.10). This is not the first time, of course, that Paul's powers of speaking have been in question; indeed in 1 Corinthians he deliberately distanced himself from any claims to rhetorical skill lest these should obscure the power of the gospel working through him,[9] and he readily admits lack of expertise in the next chapter (11.6). The charge that what he wrote in his letters was of more effect than what he tried to achieve through oratory would not have greatly troubled him: oratory was a means of persuasion he had deliberately rejected. But criticism aimed at the 'weakness of his bodily presence' was another matter. On another occasion he had to preach to the Galatians despite severe 'weakness of the flesh' (Gal. 4.13); but they, far from feeling either contempt or revulsion, received him 'as an angel of God, as Christ Jesus'. The Corinthians, however, were drawing the opposite conclusion. They imagined that Paul would be reduced to servility[10] (ταπεινός) if he met them face to face (κατὰ πρόσωπον), and could only maintain his confidence (θαρρῶ) by keeping his distance and writing 'powerful letters' (10.1,10). The news that he was still convalescent after a nearly fatal condition could well have made them feel justified in adding this charge to the more familiar one that Paul lacked the skills of rhetorical persuasion.

Paul answers these criticisms, first, by praying that he will not have to display the full confidence of his convictions when he is present with the Corinthians. If his critics think that he is hiding behind the strong words of his letters and not 'daring' (τολμῆσαι) to confront them face to face, they will soon find they are wrong – though this is not Paul's preferred style, which is to imitate 'the gentleness and magnanimity of Christ' (10.1). If he has to do so, his resources will be quite other than those which depend upon his physical condition. They will be 'weapons with the power of God' – and Paul devotes the rest of the paragraph to working out a striking simile. Besieging a town involves destroying the defences (ὀχυρώματα), confounding

---

[9] 1 Cor. 2.4.
[10] The commonest sense of ταπεινος in classical Greek e.g. Eur. *Andr.* 164–5. See *TDNT* 8.14ff.

the enemy's calculations[11] (λογισμοί) and capturing the ramparts thrown up against attack (ὕψωμα), taking prisoner (αἰχμαλωτίζειν) everyone who does not cooperate, and being ready, when the city is finally subjected (ὑπακοή), to punish any sign of rebellion (παρακοή). The simile is admittedly allegorized[12] as it goes along: the 'high ground' is arrogance over against true knowledge of God, and what are 'taken prisoner' are not men but thoughts. Nevertheless, by implication, Paul's critics are likened to a rebellious party within the city of Corinth: his response must be to besiege them and secure full submission by means of the weapons that God supplies and which have nothing to do with his physical abilities or disabilities.

But a simile must not be pressed too far. The authority which Paul has been given by God is not to create the destruction (καθαίρεσις, 10.8) involved in a siege, but to 'build up' the local church (οἰκοδομή). Paul may invoke this authority when he writes, and do so at times with some emphasis (περισσότερον); but the work of 'building up' requires an authoritative presence, and his critics, however much they may claim (like him) to 'belong to Christ', cannot deny that it is his authority, exercised when he is present himself, that has had practical results.[13] What results? To answer this, Paul has to resort again to the language of testimonials and letters of recommendation. It appears that his critics have been asking whether he had any authority to come to Corinth in the first place: was he not 'exceeding his brief' (ὑπερεκτείνομεν ἑαυτούς, 10.14)? In reply, Paul admits that there is certainly a 'standard' or 'measure' by which his work should be

---

[11] λογισμοί means logical (sometimes arithmetical) reasoning or considerations that lead to calculated action. The English word 'calculations' is a near equivalent. Lietzmann's suggestion (*HNT* 141) that it means 'sophistries' seems to be supported by no evidence, though it has made its way into AG and modern versions.

[12] In an important article, 'Antisthenes and Odysseus, and Paul at war' *HTR* 76 (1983) 143–73 = *Paul and the Popular Philosophers* (Philadelphia, 1989) 91–117, A. Malherbe has shown the prevalence of this imagery and language in philosophical debate among Stoics and Cynics. That Paul was using it metaphorically would have seemed natural to any cultivated reader; but he also takes such a different line from the philosophers that Malherbe is unable to relate his argument clearly to known philosophical debates.

[13] To make sense of verses 9–11 it seems necessary to place a stop after verse 8 and to take verse 10 as an explanatory parenthesis: 'lest I should seem to be relying on letters to frighten you into obedience (for this is what they are accusing me of), let anyone who thinks this take note of the fact that what I say in my letters I carry out in practice.'

regulated, but argues that the measure applied by his critics, by which they seek to show their own qualification for work of this kind, is totally inappropriate in his case.[14] Far from having 'exceeded his brief' by coming as far as Corinth, and far from using this as an opportunity to take credit for work done by others, Paul's hope is to see the Corinthians' faith so increased and consolidated that he can use them as a base to go still further (ὑπερέκεινα, 10.16): this is his own personal commission; his confidence does not rest on trying to appropriate someone else's 'standard' of missionary activity.[15] Confidence, in any case, derives from God and is to be attributed to God – a scriptural maxim[16] is quoted in support ('Whoever boasts let him boast in the Lord'). And self-commendation (which the critics were indulging in) was of no value compared with the commendation that comes from God.

Paul now asks permission (which he is sure of being granted)[17] for 'a little foolishness' (11.1) – an unexpected request: what use he wants to make of it becomes clear only later in the chapter. Meanwhile, the point to make is that the stakes are high. Paul's concern for the Corinthian church is like that of God for his people; and just as the prophets sometimes likened this concerned relationship to that between bridegroom and bride – God is imagined as being betrothed (Ezek. 16.8; Hos. 2.19–20) or married (Is. 54.5–6; 62.5) to Israel – so Paul thinks of the Corinthian church as 'betrothed' to Christ through his own agency, with all that this implies of exclusive commitment: no other allegiance is possible. But the very first human betrothal – that between Adam and Eve – was vulnerable to the seduction of the

---

14   The sense of verses 12–13 is certainly simplified if the last two words of 12 and the first two of 13 are omitted, following a small family of manuscripts and versions. This reading is adopted by some commentators (see Windisch ad loc.) but no explanation is offered of how the longer, much more difficult, reading would have found its way into the text.

15   Verses 12–16 are exceedingly difficult, and verse 16 seems barely grammatical. The paraphrase I have offered claims only to be a possible way of making sense of them. For detailed discussion of the possibilities, see Plummer 286–91.

16   Based on Jer. 9.22–23 LXX, but used also in 1 Cor. 1.31, suggesting that it had taken on an independent existence of its own as 'scripture'.

17   Taking ἀνέχεσθε as an indicative: after his request, an imperative would hardly be introduced by ἀλλὰ καί, pace Bl–D § 448 (6). The question is one of logic more than syntax: 'I wish you would ... but you do.'

serpent,[18] and resulted in disloyalty of thoughts and intentions. Paul is afraid of a similar corruption of the mind in the church, causing disloyalty to Christ. The signs of it are those different versions of 'Jesus' or 'Spirit' or 'gospel' which have apparently been imported into the congregation and tolerated[19] by it.

We have already noticed that the specific and targeted references to the opposition make these chapters of 2 Corinthians different from what has gone before. We are now left in no doubt that particular people are in mind; they are 'super-apostles'[20] – clearly an ironical description of men who are claiming exceptional qualifications as authorized communicators of the authentic gospel. In two respects these qualifications might seem to reflect negatively on Paul. First, their eloquence and rhetorical skills seem to put Paul's comparative lack of the persuasive arts in the shade; but Paul has dealt with this before (1 Cor. 2) and here simply makes the point that this is no way to judge a person's 'knowledge' of God.[21] Secondly, they appear to have exploited the fact that they are receiving financial support for their work: may not this mean that Paul (who received no such support) was not entitled to it, was in fact not a real 'apostle' at all? On this point we have quite a lot of background. On occasion,[22] Paul had to defend, both the right of others to receive such support, and his own right to refuse it. Here, there seems to be a further twist to the criticism

---

[18] The account in Genesis related only that the serpent deceived Eve with regard to the forbidden tree; but later tradition, both Jewish and Christian, cast the serpent in the role of a sexual seducer. This development is charted by Windisch 320–322.

[19] ἀνέχεσθε in v. 4 caused difficulties in the earliest stages of the transmission of the text. The rendering, 'you put up with it well enough' (REB) is acceptable if we understand that their toleration of the deviant preaching is a reason for Paul's fear. This means that he has to cope, not just with particular opponents, but with the congregation's acquiescence in what they are saying.

[20] The arguments against taking these 'super-apostles' as the original Jerusalem apostles are well set out by Windisch 330, and seem to me conclusive. Yet, although 'apostle' is clearly used in a much wider sense than that which was important to Paul in his own claim to the title, the term must surely retain some sense of being 'sent', of being an 'agent': Paul's opponents must have been claiming to be authorized by someone else.

[21] The second half of v. 6 is barely intelligible as it stands – hence the large number of variant readings. As it stands it is necessary to supply an object for φανερώσαντες: either 'ourselves' (cf. 5.10, 11) or some word indicating the content of this 'knowledge' (e.g. 'the full truth' REB) cf. Lietzmann 146–7.

[22] 1 Cor. 9; 2 Thess. 3.9; 2 Cor. 12.13.

he incurred: he was 'demeaning himself' (11.7) – presumably by doing manual work to bring in the necessary income.[23] Paul does not reply directly to this criticism; instead he relates how other churches have enabled him to give his services gratis to the Corinthians. He uses a vocabulary which seems to have become almost technical in this context[24] – not 'spongeing' or 'being a burden'; and he ends with an emphatic oath[25] that, at least in Achaia, he is not going to go back on this policy in which he takes such pride – an emphasis which may possibly be explained by the factor which was so prominent earlier in 2 Corinthians: if he was still convalescent it was going to be still harder for him to be self-supporting. Some might say, of course, that his refusal to accept financial support from the Corinthians simply showed how little he trusted and cared for them – an imputation to be contemptuously dismissed (11.11). At any rate, Paul has no intention of changing his policy: if he were to do so, it would enable his opponents to claim the same status as himself – and it seems as if the very thought of this riled Paul so much that he could no longer disguise his real opinion of them: false apostles and agents of Satan,[26] whose evil actions would reap their own reward.

The chapter began with Paul's appeal to be allowed 'a little foolishness'. There was then a digression, but now (11.16) he comes back to it. This foolishness involves an element of boasting, which he admits is 'fleshly' and not 'godly' (11.18), but which the boasting of his opponents stings him into indulging. We must not be misled by this word 'flesh': it can cover anything which is not 'godly' or 'spiritual', even the stoical endurance of ridicule, insult and maltreatment which it was the pride of philosophers to cultivate in themselves and their pupils.[27] It was this kind of philosophical endurance, in fact, that Paul's

---

[23]   R. F. Hock, *The Social Context of Paul's Ministry* (Philadelphia, 1980), assembles evidence to illustrate the social consequences of a teacher doing manual work. The point was in fact controversial: not everyone disapproved of it. But Paul may well have known or assumed that his opponents did so.

[24]   I have drawn attention to Paul's use of this apparently conventional vocabulary in 'The Workman is Worthy of his Hire' *NovT* 24 (1982) 209–221 on 215–6.

[25]   'The truth of Christ is in me' (11.10) – correctly identified as an oath by Windisch ad loc.

[26]   The idea that Satan disguised himself as an angel of light is found in the *Life of Adam and Eve* 9.

[27]   This is clearest in 10.3 where, using weapons other than those of the 'flesh', Paul is ready to attack all calculated and overweening opposition to the knowledge of God.

opponents were boasting of, and in which Paul is about to show himself greatly superior. In this contest it was of course a disgrace to own up to any weakness.[28] If Paul had recently done so (which could well have been a consequence of his near-death experience) he would be aware that in his opponents' terms he might seem to have lost his reputation for stamina. This, of course was not the real issue: the power which sustained him was infinitely greater than could be obtained from a course of philosophy. Nevertheless, at the risk of appearing 'foolish', it was worth showing that, even on their own ground, he was more than equal to his opponents.

It is doubtless for this reason that the famous list of tribulations which follows, unlike those earlier in the letter, is remarkably detailed and specific. It would not have made the point merely to say in general terms what he had been through. At this 'fleshly' level, he needed to show his superiority by the sheer cumulative weight of a whole variety of sufferings. Not that the list is necessarily exact in every detail. Any such recital of personal vicissitudes is liable to be a little vague about the precise number of occasions on which a certain deprivation was endured and to lump together experiences which may have greatly varied in severity: and piling on case after case of apparently heroic endurance was a rhetorical device from which Paul may well have drawn perhaps unconscious inspiration.[29] It is therefore not necessary to think that, even if we had more information about Paul, we could find events in his life to fill out every category he mentions – imprisonments, river-dangers, sleepless nights and so forth – with more than one severe instance, or even with a serious instance at all. On the other hand, when he works into the list references to specific and unusual tribulations the rhetoric gives place to solid information, and

---

[28] Verse 21 causes the commentators great difficulty: who is saying 'that we have been weak'? Is 'a matter of disgrace' descriptive or ironical? I follow the grammatically simplest rendering, taking ὡς ὅτι as the content of λέγω: 'It is to my disgrace that I say that I have been weak.'

[29] This is illustrated by R. Hodgson, 'Paul the Apostle and First Century Tribulation Lists' *ZNW* 74 (1983) 59–80 from a number of examples. Note especially Plutarch, *De Alexandri magna fortuna* 327c: '... moreover, the conditions of the expedition itself, storms, droughts, depths of rivers, the heights of the Birdless Mountains, harsh living conditions, changes of petty rulers and treacherous inter-relationships; besides all this, the circumstances before the expedition ...'.

we find ourselves learning things about Paul which are known from
no other source. We learn a certain amount also about his opponents:
they are Hebrews, Israelites and descendants of Abraham,[30] no less
(but also no more) than Paul is. They also are (or claim to be) 'servants
of Christ', which is not just a pious term of speech, but implies a
claim to be acting in Christ's name with some authority.[31] Paul replies
with an account of what this 'service' really involves: his own record
shows him to have risen far further than they in the ranks of such
'servants'.

'Labours – imprisonments – beatings – mortal dangers'.[32] The recital
is still general, though rising in severity. The specifics are filled in by
the sentences that follow. 'Forty strokes save one' was the maximum
Jewish judicial punishment short of the death penalty: to have endured
– and survived – it five times must have been exceptional by any
standards, particularly if (as it seems) Paul submitted to it voluntarily.[33]
The same goes for three 'beatings with rods', one of the severest
punishments under Roman law:[34] as a Roman citizen, Paul was
technically exempt from it, but whether he chose not to be or had no
opportunity to claim exemption (as seems to have been the case at
Philippi: Acts 16.22) we do not know.[35] 'Stoning', again, was normally
fatal, being the regular form of capital punishment under Jewish law;
but since such executions were not permitted in Roman provinces[36]
the episode is more likely to have been an attempted lynching such as

---

[30] On the difference between these titles, see Martin 373–4. It can be argued that they are
on an ascending theological scale: 'Hebrews', an ethnic designation; 'Israelites', an
indication of national and religious identity; 'seed of Abraham', a community of faith of
which Christians as well as Jews are members.

[31] Cf. J. Collins, *Diakonia* (New York, OUP, 1991) 218–20 (on 2 Cor. 9.12).

[32] ἐν θανάτοις πολλάκις. If this is to be taken literally, meaning a whole series of near-
death experiences comparable with that in 1.8, it is clearly fatal to my whole argument.
But it is a perfectly natural way of referring to circumstances so dangerous they might
have caused death, but which Paul was able to face without despairing of escape.

[33] A. E. Harvey 'Forty Strokes Save One', in A. E. Harvey ed., *Alternative Approaches to NT
Study* (London, 1985) 79–96. For the details of the punishment, see the commentaries
and S. Gallas, 'Fünfmal vierzig weniger einen …' *ZNW* 81 (1990) 180–191.

[34] Mommsen, *Röm. Strafrecht* 983.

[35] See examples cited by Windisch 356.

[36] The argument whether this was the case in Jerusalem, summarized in HJP 2.219–23,
does not affect the general rule governing Roman provincial administration, on which
see A. N. Sherwin-White, *Roman Society and Roman Law in the NT* (Oxford, 1963) 36.

Paul underwent at Lystra according to Acts 14.19. As for shipwreck and the other hazards of travelling, these will have come to Paul willy-nilly in the course of his missionary work (though *three* shipwrecks, or four if we count the subsequent one on the way to Rome, must surely have been exceptional, even for a professional sailor); whereas some of his ordeals, such as fasting, may have been self-imposed,[37] and his daily anxiety for his churches was a consequence of the particular role that he had adopted, that of travelling apostle and pastor to a widely separated network of Christian communities. Indeed this was more than ordinary anxiety: the occasions on which those churches and their members had suffered harassment and persecution were a fiery ordeal both for them and for Paul himself, who carried the responsibility for their being subjected to it.[38]

Coming from a philosopher, such a catalogue of ordeals successfully endured would be testimony to his strength of endurance, his constancy and equanimity.[39] Paul has allowed himself to be led into this degree of 'boasting' by his opponents, but now reverses the terms of the competition by protesting that his ordeals have been marks, not of his strength, but of his 'weakness'. The list has shown that it would be absurd to criticize him for lack of stamina; but equally the stamina itself has nothing to do with the real qualifications of the 'servant of Christ'; the only grounds on which one can claim *this* title is that of sharing the weakness and humiliation of Christ. It is thus, perhaps, that we should understand the rather unexpected little episode recounted in the final sentence. Being smuggled through a city wall in a basket had been a lucky escape, but it hardly brought credit to Paul. Indeed, he may mention it expressly to symbolize the degree of humiliation he constantly suffered,[40] in contrast to the power of God which could 'demolish strongholds' (10.4).

[37] 'Sleepless nights' in the sense of vigils, may also have been voluntary: cf. Martin 380.

[38] In a series of articles (*CBQ* 36 (1974) 193–202; *CBQ* 37 (1975) 500–526; *CBQ* 42 (1980) 216–227) M. Barré has argued persuasively for a consistent meaning of eschatological trial in the cluster of words ἀσθένης, σκάνδαλον, πυροῦν.

[39] Cf. the *constantia, firmitas* etc. commended by Seneca: John T. Fitzgerald, *Cracks in an Earthen Vessel* 62–5.

[40] In a famous article ('The Conflict of Educational Aims in NT Thought', *Journal of Christian Education* 9 (1966) 32–45) E. A. Judge saw Paul's account as a parody of the achievement of a Roman soldier in scaling a city wall and winning the *corona muralis*.

Since the end of the Middle Ages we have had the advantage of the word 'mystical' with which to describe the experience which Paul now goes on to report. By its very nature, such experience (when genuine) can hardly give rise to 'boasting': the reality to which it gives access is too overwhelming for the subject to think of taking credit for it. Paul's use of the word καυχᾶσθαι here illustrates the wider range of meaning it has than any English equivalent. There could be no question of boasting: but a mystical experience could legitimately give rise to 'confidence' and a sense of authority in speaking of the things of God. Being so subjective, and essentially incommunicable (an oxymoron like 'words that cannot be uttered' is typical of mystical experiences), no amount of such experiences could be decisive: authority to speak and act must rest on more objective qualifications (12.6–7). But the fact of having had such experiences is something that must occasionally be told to others, and in this case was a further ground for Paul's self-confidence when confronted by the claims of his opponents.

We cannot of course know what Paul experienced. The most we can do is enquire into the resources which his religion and his culture offered him for giving it some shape and enabling him to communicate it, however vaguely, to others.[41] When we compare other accounts of visionary experiences in Jewish literature, the very first thing we notice is that the writer never allowed himself to appear as the subject, but either wrote anonymously and ascribed the experience to a figure of the past (e.g. 'The Ascension of Isaiah') or else wrote pseudonymously in the person of Daniel, Enoch or some other venerable seer. This tradition, which was matched by a (possibly first century) rabbinic rule forbidding public discussion of such things,[42] makes it less surprising that Paul should show such reticence in acknowledging the experience as his own. We notice, secondly, that the notions of being 'caught up', of ascending through successive 'heavens', and of finding oneself in 'paradise', are all part of the visionary vocabulary of the time, though we cannot expect the usage to have been sufficiently consistent for us to be able to say with certainty whether the 'third

---

[41] An important contribution to such an enquiry is made by A. F. Segal, *Paul the Convert* (Yale University Press, 1990) 58ff.

[42] Segal *op cit* 58–9: no rabbinic reference is given.

heaven', like the 'seventh' in other authors,[43] was also the 'highest', that is, in immediate proximity to God himself. All we can say for certain on the basis of this passage is that Paul genuinely had an experience which we would now call 'mystical' and that he used language and concepts that were current in his time in order to convey something of its significance. If (as is possible) his opponents were claiming some form of supernatural revelation or authorization for themselves, it was reasonable for Paul to give a reticent account of his own experience in reply. Such a reply could indicate the basis of his confidence without laying him open to a charge of 'boasting'.

Yet Paul sees a danger. He *might* have been tempted by this experience, if not to boast, at least to claim superiority on the basis of his heavenly visions, to be improperly 'elated'. This possibility suggests to him a way of making sense of his 'thorn in the flesh': the continual and humiliating 'punishment' this gave him was an effective antidote to any feeling of superiority. I argued at the beginning of this study[44] that there are good reasons why it is impossible to know exactly what this 'thorn' consisted of: it could have been a chronic illness or disability;[45] equally (so far as the language goes) it could have been a particularly persistent and noxious form of harassment.[46] Either way, Paul received an oracular response[47] to his prayer, enigmatic in itself, but becoming ever clearer in the light of his perception of the significance and value of bearing such sufferings 'in Christ'. 'Weakness', whether induced by physical infirmity and exhaustion or by the attacks of enemies, is precisely the vehicle by which the 'power' of Christ is manifested. All such ordeals – which are now summarized in a few simple words (12.10) – may be borne 'on behalf of Christ'. When this is so, apparent weakness becomes strength.

---

[43] For an account of these, see Martin 401–2: three, five, seven and ten all occur in Jewish literature.

[44] See above pp. 10–11.

[45] Worked out in detail by K. Seybold and U. Mueller, *Sickness and Healing* (Abingdon Press, 1978–81) 175ff.

[46] M. Barré, *CBQ* 42 (1980) 216–227. See above n. 38.

[47] H. D. Betz, 'Eine Christus-Apologie bei Paulus' (2 Kor. 12.7–10)', *ZThK* 66 (1969) 288–305, illustrates the oracular character of the answer to Paul's prayer, especially from Delphic oracles; cf. also Seybold and Mueller (n. 45), 177–8.

At the beginning of chapter 11 Paul asked permission to indulge in 'a little foolishness', namely, in a recital of achievements and attributes which showed him to be at least the equal of those who criticized him or who claimed to be 'super-apostles'. This recital is now completed: 'I have had my turn of foolishness.' It was something he had been forced into – and here his criticism is turned directly upon the recipients of this letter: it was they who should have recited his qualifications to these self-styled 'apostles', instead of leaving it to him. Even if they could say he had no positive skills and abilities (such as a gift of rhetoric), he was certainly not inferior to them in that many-sided 'endurance' which many might regard as a fruit of philosophical detachment but which was actually (for other reasons) a mark of a true apostle – as were also more supernatural feats ('signs and wonders and powers', 12.12), which Paul does not normally lay claim to but which had apparently attended his work in Corinth. It was nonsense to suggest that the church in Corinth had had less than its fair share of demonstrations of its founder's authority (12.13).

Unless, of course, they were still feeling slighted by Paul's refusal to accept any financial support from them. Paul has already explained and defended his policy on this a number of times. He now declares that he will continue in the same way on his third visit, taking care not to 'sponge'[48] on them: if they still think he is doing them an 'injustice', they will simply have to forgive him. But the matter evidently remained sensitive, and Paul comes back to it with yet another argument to justify his attitude. He has more than once described his relationship with his Christian converts as that of a parent with a child – a mother who brings to birth a baby (Gal. 4.19) or a father who begets (1 Cor. 4.15; Phlm.10) or cares for (1 Cor. 4.14) his children. He now applies this to the question of material support. The analogy was of course double-edged. It was a fundamental axiom of the Jewish culture and indeed of ancient morality in general that children should support their parents in old age or infirmity;[49] and

---

[48] Jerome *Ep.* 121. 10.4 tells us that this was an expression local to Cilicia, meaning 'to be a burden'.

[49] See Philo's discussion, *De Decalago* 112–120; also the many passages from pagan and Jewish literature cited by P. van der Horst, *The Sentences of Pseudo-Phocylides* (Leiden, 1978) 116.

this would hardly have helped Paul to claim total independence from his 'children' in this respect. But it was also true that it is parents who amass capital for the sake of passing it on to their children, not children for the sake of their parents.[50] So Paul could argue (we must suppose)[51] that in so far as he had got the 'capital' (in fact contributed by 'children' from other churches!) out of which to pay his own expenses it would be wrong for him, as 'father', to receive a levy from the 'capital' of his converts when he visited them. But in any case, of course, this parent-child relationship affected far more than financial arrangements. In Greek and Latin,[52] as in English, one did not only speak of spending money. One could spend or 'be spent' oneself – which exactly described what Paul was doing for the Corinthians. Surely this should not mean that he was loved the less in return!

But given that Paul was laying no charge on the Corinthians for his expenses, might he not be covertly subtracting it from the sum raised in the collection? Of all the charges made against Paul this appears to be the most damaging: he and his associates had actually been dishonest in their administration of the money. Paul's reply is simply to refer again to the formal arrangements made for the collection. The person entrusted with the 'commission' (παρεκάλεσα, 12.18)[53] was Titus, whose record with the Corinthians was above suspicion; but to make doubly sure, Titus had been accompanied by an official representative of the other churches involved,[54] whose standing was also impeccable (8.18–19). With three agents of such reputation and probity, what possibility was there of any of them having manipulated the funds?

---

[50] The passage cited from Philo by Windisch and others (*Vit. Mos.* 2.245) is not strictly relevant: Philo is saying that it is 'unnatural' for parents to *inherit* from their children (if they die first). But the principle is obvious enough.

[51] Commentators regularly see the difficulty that Paul *did* accept support from others among his 'children' but do not really face the weakness of the analogy itself, which would normally work the other way.

[52] Plut. *Galb.* 17; Seneca *Prov.* 5.4 (boni viri ... impenduntur).

[53] See above pp. 83 n. 10 and 85 n. 16.

[54] 'I sent with him the brother'. The article here is plainly anaphoric (BD § 252), 'the brother whom you know, whom I mentioned before'. This is the clearest cross-reference in 2 Cor.: the phrase is meaningless except in relation to 8.18.

'Have you been thinking for some time that I am defending myself to you?' (12.19).[55] Paul might properly have felt uneasy about appearing to resort to self-defence. It implied, first, that he was on the defensive – which indeed he was: but this did not mean that he was willing to come down and fight on the ground of his opponents. It implied, also, that he might be using some of the rhetorical techniques associated with a formal 'apology',[56] techniques which might have strengthened the argument but at the same time raised the question whether he was completely sincere. So he protests, first, his sincerity: everything he says is 'before God' and 'in Christ'. Secondly, his motive is not his own reputation but the health of the Corinthian community. And to press the point home, he confronts them with the stark personal consequences[57] of failing to heed him. If, when he comes, he and they find themselves still unreconciled, the result will be the very opposite of 'building up' – and Paul indulges in a typical moralist's catalogue[58] of baleful consequences. There is also the danger that he will once again be 'humiliated' (did he fear a repetition of debilitating illness?) and be unable to do more than lament[59] the lack of repentance among those who had caused dissension by their sexually permissive way of life.

Undeniably, Paul has been on the defensive. Attacks have been made on his integrity which have to be answered. Some of these have been on the relatively crude level of financial manipulation; others have touched deeper questions of his credibility and authority as an apostle, and I have suggested that reports of the nearly fatal episode recorded in 1.8 could have been at least one of the factors that brought such criticisms to a head. One way or another the situation between Paul and the church in Corinth has begun to resemble a trial. Accusations

---

[55] 'To you' may bear some emphasis, as Windisch and others note, but hardly to the extent of the REB's 'it is you we are addressing …'.

[56] Aristotle, *Rhet.* 3.15.1.

[57] This seems easier than to suppose, with most commentators, that these causes of dissension were already present in the community, causing a question whether they characterized the same group as those in 12.21.

[58] For examples, see H. Lietzmann, *An die Römer* (*HNT*, 1928) 35–7 (Exkurs).

[59] πενθεῖν means properly (as translators and commentators tend to forget) grieving over some *loss*. Rather than a general feeling of regret at these people's unreformed way of life we probably ought to think of Paul grieving over them as 'lost' for the world to come.

have been made and answered. But there was one feature of the Jewish legal process which was totally unlike ours.[60] If a defendant was found to be innocent, the matter might not rest there: an immediate reversal of roles was possible, the former defendant could become the accuser, and charges that had been levelled against him could be used to discredit and condemn his opponents. In the words of a rabbinic saying, 'Woe to him whose advocate turns accuser!'[61]

It is this reversal of roles which seems to be in Paul's mind when he comes to speak of the visit he proposes to make to Corinth (13.1). When he arrives, what kind of confrontation will it be? That it can be thought of as a legal one is made clear by the reference to court proceedings. 'A charge must be established on the evidence of two or three witnesses.' This proposition from Deuteronomy (19.15) laid down a fundamental rule of procedure: unsupported testimony was not acceptable. When the rule is quoted elsewhere in the New Testament[62] it marks the point at which a private dispute becomes a matter for public arbitration: from now on strict rules of evidence will apply. It appears to have the same force here. It is as if Paul is saying, 'My next visit will be the occasion for our dispute to be publicly settled.' But how would the rule have worked in this case? So long as Paul was the defendant, it was his accusers who needed more than one witness against him – and of course this would have been no problem for them: there was presumably a whole group of them prepared to speak for the case against Paul. But now suppose the tables were turned: Paul will 'bring a case' against his detractors. It will then be he, not they, who needs corroborative testimony. To whom can he turn as a witness for the prosecution? In such a situation there was always one recourse open to a plaintiff. If there was no one available to support his case, he could take an extreme step: he could 'call God to witness',

---

[60] I have developed this point in relation to John 5.31 and 8.14ff. in *Jesus on Trial* (London, 1976) 57–8.

[61] Midrash Lev. R. 30.6.

[62] In Mt. 18.16 and 1 Tim. 5.19 it is a rule for an actual judicial hearing, In John 8.17 it is a reminder (as here) of what is involved when a dispute is thought of in legal terms. Commentators have laboured to answer the question who or what Paul's 'witnesses' were. Were they the visits? Or the letter? But on my interpretation the question becomes irrelevant.

that is, he could swear an oath.[63] Of course this was not to be done lightly. Swearing a false oath (it was believed) would certainly be punished by God. One would not take the risk if one had the smallest doubt about the truth of one's own case. But if one did so it would settle the matter: one's opponents would not willingly incur the consequences of challenging a statement corroborated by a solemn oath. One's second 'witness' – God – was decisive.

It is in the light of this that we can best understand Paul's unusual expression, 'Christ speaking in me' (13.3). His next visit would be critical. He would have a case against his critics, and the issue must be decided once and for all. It would be to all intents and purposes a trial. But who would be the witness on Paul's side? He could of course simply rely on an oath: he could 'call God to witness'. But there was a more personal, and more 'Christian', way of doing this. Again and again Paul has spoken of his intense union and solidarity with Christ – a living presence constantly with him. *He* would be Paul's witness when it came to the trial – and would of course settle the matter: Paul was not going to 'spare' either those who had actually offended, or those who had taken their side, by deferring the issue any longer.[64]

But of course this was really only another way of stating the dispute between them. That Paul could appeal to Christ speaking as a witness in him and for him was precisely what they had been calling into question. For them, Christ seemed to be a source of strength; but Paul had been discovered in a state of weakness. How then could Paul claim to have Christ 'in' him? To which the answer was in terms of what we now think of as authentic Pauline theology: union with Christ involves identification with him both in his crucifixion and in his resurrection. It is equally intense whether in shared weakness or divinely imparted strength. And the strength would be apparent when Paul confronted those who had sought to bring a case against him. His case would be unanswerable.

---

[63] A. E. Harvey, *Jesus on Trial* 57. Cf. Z. W. Falk, *Introduction to Jewish Law of the Second Commonwealth* I (Leiden, 1972) 129–132.

[64] In Jewish law (the tradition goes back to Simeon b. Shetah, *Makkoth* 5b), conniving or scheming witnesses were equally culpable. Cf. Falk op. cit. 127.

This legal language was of course only a manner of speaking. Paul was not expecting to appear before any tribunal: the point was rather to stress that now, as always, Paul was not speaking and acting on his own authority but was an authorized representative of Christ. If they doubted him, they would be doubting Christ himself: Christ was 'speaking in him'. But this adversarial way of depicting the issue between Paul and the Corinthians raised an awkward question.[65] Christ was 'in' Paul, speaking for him and corroborating his case against those who had attacked him. But was he not also 'in' his converts, those for whom (as he says elsewhere) he has laboured until Christ should be 'formed in them' (Gal. 4.19)? And if Christ were 'in' them also, how could he give evidence for both parties in the dispute? In other words, how could Paul claim to have Christ speaking for him without the unwelcome consequence of having to deny that his converts 'had' Christ at all? Christ could hardly be on both sides of the argument. If Paul were to prevail, would it mean that the Corinthians were estranged, not just from him, but from Christ?

Clearly, the question whether the Corinthians stood firmly 'in the faith', whether 'Christ was among them' (13.5), could not depend on the issue of this particular dispute. It was something they would have intuitive knowledge of and which they could put to the test by self-examination. It could be known even by its fruits in their moral conduct (13.7). Such testing could be applied to Paul, and he hopes he would pass it; if they passed it themselves – which was the most important thing – the consequence might even be that Paul would be found wanting: for the sake of their life in Christ he would even accept this. What was at stake was the truth. The question throughout has been whether the evidences of Paul's 'weakness' (among which, as I have suggested from the beginning, may have been his near-death experience), as compared with their apparent 'strength', called into question his credibility as an apostle. His own interior journey had enabled him to find this moment of extreme weakness, not one of humiliation and loss of confidence, but of encouragement and joy. By

---

[65] This implication, which greatly clarifies the argument of 13.5–10, seems to have been missed by commentators.

writing of it before his arrival, he hoped to avoid the kind of confrontation which would involve appealing to the authority with which Christ had invested him. This would inevitably result in a decisive judgement against them, the very opposite of the purpose for which he possessed this authority in the first place, which was to 'build up' a congregation, not 'tear it down'. His prayer is rather that whatever was amiss should be 'put back in place', and that they should receive that consolation and encouragement (παρακαλεῖν) which has been the theme of the letter from the beginning.

Chapter 6

Renewal through Suffering

I have argued that Paul's account of his near-death experience in 2 Corinthians 1.8–10 is to be taken seriously as the record of a critical episode in his life. Whether caused by sickness, accident or persecution – and the conventions of his time would not have encouraged him to recount the details we should so dearly like to have – it is likely to have had profound consequences for him, both in terms of his physical ability to continue in the style of activity and economic independence to which he was accustomed and on which he prided himself, and in terms of his credibility in the eyes of others and his confidence in himself as an authorized apostle, a bearer of a gospel of salvation and a member of the privileged generation that would live to see the return of Christ. The way in which he came to terms with it, and the positive value which it enabled him to find in suffering, are the key (as I have tried to show) to the intense and sometimes tortuous paragraphs in chapters 4 and 5; and I have given a somewhat summary account of the argument of the rest of 2 Corinthians in order to indicate the numerous other passages where its influence may perhaps be seen.

It may be helpful at this point to set out the biographical sequence which I have been pre-supposing. Paul's first visit to Corinth, during which he founded the church there, lasted at least a year. When he left, he went to Ephesus for some two to three years. It was during this period at Ephesus that the Corinthian letters were written. It was here, therefore, that Paul suffered 'the tribulation we endured in Asia', an experience which (I have argued) can be detected behind much of the writing of 2 Corinthians. Do the relative precision of these data (52–55 CE, Ephesus), and their connection with the extant letters, allow us to say any more about the experience itself?

We know that soon after Paul's arrival in Ephesus he received letters and visits from Corinth which caused him to write 1 Corinthians. In the course of that letter he referred to 'fighting with wild beasts at Ephesus' (15.32). I have already suggested that this is hardly to be taken literally; people who were thrown to the lions did not return alive to continue their correspondence. But even when taken as a figure of speech it must have meant something quite severe. Could it have been the 'tribulation' Paul refers to in 2 Corinthians?

This seems very unlikely. 'We do not want you to be ignorant of the tribulations we endured …' is hardly a natural way of referring to something which has been mentioned in a previous letter. But there is a more significant reason. The 'wild beast' experience, Paul had said, would have seemed meaningless apart from faith in the resurrection of the dead. 'What profit was there for me in it?' Only the resurrection gave any point to the incessant dangers and hardships Paul was enduring; in themselves they were entirely without value, and would have amounted to an argument for withdrawing from the whole enterprise had it not been for the reward guaranteed by resurrection. This is in total contrast to the way in which the near-death experience of 2 Corinthians is found to be a means of inner renewal and intense solidarity with Christ.

If, then, the 'tribulation in Asia' took place subsequent to the writing of 1 Corinthians, do we know anything about Paul's later months at Ephesus that might throw light on it? There is nothing of this kind to be learnt from Acts, which passes very rapidly over Paul's stay; and the riot which forced him to leave seems not to have resulted in any injury to him. Our only source of information is 2 Corinthians itself. We have been concentrating on the evidence this provides for the working out of the crucial near-death experience, and the criticisms and attacks on Paul's character that it may have provoked. But the situation was complicated by a crisis of another kind. To resolve the disciplinary problem that had already been tackled in 1 Corinthians, Paul was compelled, possibly to pay a further short visit in person,[1] and certainly to write a letter which caused him personal pain and considerable apprehension about how it would be received. This anxiety prevented him from making a further visit to Corinth in case he should find the situation still unresolved; it also made him too restless to continue with the promising work he had started in Troas. His relief at the news that the letter had resulted, not in further bitterness and confrontation, but in repentance and reconciliation, was such that his

[1] See p. 38, n. 12.

recollection of that moment produced one of the warmest and most confident paragraphs in his entire correspondence.

Clearly this episode was one that caused considerable tension at the time and, in its outcome, greatly deepened the relationship between Paul and the Corinthian Christians. Our difficulty with 2 Corinthians is that this scenario, recounted from the vantage point of its intensely rewarding resolution, does not account for those passages at certain points in the letter, and in particular in chapters 10 to 13, where Paul is distinctly and sometimes even bitterly on the defensive *at the time of writing.* His qualifications for his work were being questioned, his probity doubted, his skills derided, his authority challenged. 'Super-apostles' were ranged against him, and he had to reprimand the Corinthians for paying respect and attention to them. As so often in the Pauline letters, the detail of these attacks and criticisms, and the character of his opponents, remain tantalizingly indistinct, and I have not attempted to make them less so: there are already whole libraries of speculation on the subject. I have simply suggested one factor – the near-death experience – which could (according to the understanding of such things at the time) have caused something of a crisis in Paul's credibility as an apostle or at least greatly exacerbated criticisms that were already being made of him on other grounds. This experience is unlikely to have occurred during the previous crisis: Paul does not bring the two together at any point in the letter; in which case we must assume that it took place after his return to Ephesus from Macedonia, where he had met Titus and received the good news of reconciliation. But, equally, it cannot have been immediately before he wrote 2 Corinthians; there must have been time for the criticisms it aroused against Paul to have reached Corinth and for the 'super-apostles' to have used them to challenge Paul's authority. We must place it therefore some time in the last year of his stay in Ephesus. A few months after it happened, Paul wrote 2 Corinthians (or at least substantial parts of it). I have attempted to show the influence which it had on the writing of that letter.

But if the experience had such crucial significance for Paul, then it clearly marks an important point in his biography, and might be expected to have affected his thinking and writing on subsequent occasions. I shall not have made my case unless I can show that it found expression in letters subsequent to 2 Corinthians but is absent from all previous letters. Here of course we have some difficulty with our sources. In what order were Paul's letters written? Not only that, but is it certain that the various parts of 2 Corinthians were originally in the order in which they now appear? It has been argued, for instance, that chapters 8 and 9 were originally quite separate 'letters of commendation',[2] and a case can be made out (even if it is not widely accepted) for chapters 10–13 having been the 'sorrowful letter' referred to earlier[3] and therefore having been written *before* the experience which (I have been arguing) influenced some of the expressions they contain. This is a serious objection; and it cannot be obviated simply by pointing to the greater weight of scholarly opinion on the side of reading the various sections of 2 Corinthians in the order in which they are printed:[4] *any* uncertainty about their place in Paul's biography makes it unwise to use these chapters as evidence for the working out of an experience which may not have occurred before they were written. To which I can only reply that if, by taking these chapters as they come, I have been able to show some consistency of thought and argument, then this may itself be a reason to accept their traditional place in Paul's correspondence; but in any case the allusions I have traced in them to the near-death experience, though plausible and occasionally illuminating, are in no case certain and could be explained in other ways if these passages turned out to belong to an earlier stage in Paul's life.

There is however a rather more serious challenge to be met. It may be granted that there is nothing in either letter to the Thessalonians which indicates the understanding of suffering which Paul achieved by the time he wrote 2 Corinthians, and that 1 Corinthians (as I argued in chapter 1) quite definitely expresses a traditional and unoriginal view of it compared with that of the later letter. But there is one other letter which *may* be earlier than 2 Corinthians, and which contains a highly suggestive expression:

---

[2] H. D. Betz, *2 Corinthians 8 and 9; A Commentary on Two Administrative Letters of the Apostle Paul.*

[3] E.g. A. Plummer, ICC (Edinburgh, 1915) xxviiiff; F. Watson, '2 Cor. 10–13 and Paul's Painful Visit to the Corinthians', *JTS* 35 (1984) 324–46.

[4] Listed by Martin, xlii.

I bear the marks of Jesus branded on my body … (Gal. 6.17)

The dating of Galatians is notoriously difficult: much depends on whether it was written to North or South Galatia and how it relates to the conferences in Acts 11 and 15.[5] A *possible* date is close to the writing of Romans, when Paul was in Macedonia (Acts 20.1–3);[6] but an earlier date is on the whole more probable (it could even be Paul's first surviving letter[7]), in which case the reference to the stigmata of Jesus long before the near-death experience demands some explanation. May it not show that Paul had found a positive significance in suffering at quite an early stage? To this, however, there is a simple reply. The way in which Paul had come to find a meaning in suffering after his experience of nearly dying was in the 'renewal' of the 'inner man'. But in Galatians he was talking about outward visible marks on his body. Whether these were simply scars acquired as a result of professing Jesus,[8] or whether he was thinking of them as 'branding' him as a slave of Jesus,[9] the emphasis is undoubtedly on the external signs of suffering. It can hardly be said that the phrase anticipates the deep internalization of suffering we find in 2 Corinthians 4.[10]

More important is the question whether reflection on the same experience can be found in letters that can be presumed to have been written later than 2 Corinthians. It has to be said at once that there is no direct allusion to it; from which it might be inferred that it cannot have been as crucial an event in Paul's life as I have been suggesting: if it was, surely Paul would have referred to it more often. But we have

---

5   See the full account of these possibilities in E. de W. Burton, *Galatians*, ICC (Edinburgh, 1921) xliv–liii.

6   Burton, *Galatians*, xlix.

7   As is assumed by the more conservative wing of scholarship, e.g. F. F. Bruce, *Paul: Apostle of the Free Spirit* (Exeter, 1997) 475.

8   Perhaps as a result of severe flogging: A. E. Harvey, 'Forty Strokes Save One' in A. E. Harvey, ed., *Alternative Approaches to NT Study* (London, 1985) 93–4.

9   See the passages cited by J. B. Lightfoot, *Galatians* 225 and P. W. van der Horst, *The Sentences of Pseudo-Phocylides* 256–7.

10   And the same is surely true of Gal. 2.19, 'I have been crucified with Christ.' That paragraph (Gal. 2.15–21) is not about suffering at all, it is about a Christian's proper attitude to 'observances of the law'. Christ's crucifixion, we read in 3.13, made him a 'curse' so far as the law was concerned, and so purchased *our* freedom from the law. And we appropriate this by 'being crucified with him'.

to remember a point which was made at the outset with regard to autobiographical references in general. Paul did not write to his churches simply to tell them interesting things about himself. If he mentioned things from his past, he did so in order to make a point, to answer criticism or to support a claim. In 2 Corinthians, as we have seen, he found it important to dwell on his recent experience in order to scotch any false inferences that his critics might be drawing from it. But we should not expect references to it if there was no such point at issue.

This needs to be borne in mind when we turn to Romans 6.1–11, a passage in which there are clear echoes of 2 Corinthians 4. 'If we have become identified with him in the likeness of his death, so we shall be with him in his resurrection' (6.5), 'let us walk in *newness* of life' (6.4) '... has been crucified with him' (6.6). Now it is certainly arguable that these echoes are merely verbal and coincidental. The immediate context is a reference to baptism. If there is a sense in which Christians 'die' with Christ, this is not by virtue of carrying about the dying condition (νέκρωσις) of Christ in their physical sufferings but simply as a result of baptism; and the idea of 'being crucified with Christ' is already familiar from Galatians 2.19, where it springs, not from a contemplation of Christ's sufferings on the cross, but from a perception of the cross as a sign of total distancing from the law, of 'dying to the law' as Jesus did. Moreover the drift of the argument in this section of Romans is to do, not with suffering, but with sin; and the identification with Christ signifies a death to 'the body of sin', not a means to renewal through suffering. Yet the presupposition of the whole passage is that identification with Christ's death is a reality for the Christian. It takes place, certainly, through baptism (6.3); it takes place also through a new quality of ethical behaviour (6.4) so that our 'dying' with Christ frees us from the power of sin and its necessary consequence, death. But that it takes place also through suffering is stated explicitly in 8.17: 'fellow-heirs with Christ, so long as we suffer with him so that we may also be glorified with him' – where the juxtaposition of suffering with 'glory' is an unmistakable echo of the argument of 2 Corinthians 3–4. Paul, that is to say, has a number of ways of expressing and accounting for this identification of the Christian with Christ. But the absolute conviction with which he does so is most easily explained if it was born of that experience of sharing the 'dying' of Christ right up to the point of (as it seemed) certain death which inspired the writing of 2 Corinthians.

But now it has to be asked whether all this is true of *any* suffering, or only that which is specifically endured by a Christian, or even by a special Christian such as an apostle. Or (to put it another way), was it necessary that the suffering should be such as could be described as θλῖψις, as a consequence of the inevitable resistance which the world puts up to the gospel and its messengers? What of those tribulations listed by Paul which were due (as we would say) to natural causes, such as shipwreck and dangers of river and desert (11.25–6)? Is there a special category of sufferings which create our identity with Christ and qualify us to be 'fellow heirs' with him? It would be hard to find an answer to this in Paul,[11] and this is probably because the question is not correctly posed. It is not a matter of asking what kind of sufferings are most easily understood as being borne 'with' Christ; it is a question of what explanation is adequate to the bearing of any particular suffering. We have seen that in certain circumstances Paul was satisfied with the conventional wisdom: suffering is a test or a discipline;[12] it will be compensated richly in the life to come.[13] It was also widely understood that following Jesus, like adhering to any noble but unpopular cause, might involve persecution, but that by its very nature such suffering could be endured joyfully, even if it led to martyrdom.[14] But none of these explanations had been adequate to account for the pain, the humiliation, the disability and the dashing of long-held hopes involved (for Paul) in the experience of standing on the very brink of death. Instead, he had discovered in it and through it a solidarity with Christ in *his* sufferings and an interior renewal in counterpoint to the battering of his outward person which meant that there was now no suffering beyond the reach of the 'consolation' offered by God through Christ.

---

[11] Cf. M. D. Hooker, 'Interchange in Christ', *JTS* 22 (1971), 349–61 at 359: 'It is very doubtful whether Paul would have distinguished between one type of suffering and another.'

[12] 1 Cor. 10.13; 11.32; 2 Cor. 6.9 παιδευόμενοι καὶ μὴ θανατούμενοι. Cf. Prov. 3.11–12.

[13] Rom. 8.18; 1 Cor. 15.30–31.

[14] 1 Thess. 1.6; Phil. 1.29; 1 Pet. *passim*.

This discussion has cleared the ground for approaching the crucial passage in Philippians (3.10),

> to know Christ and the power of his resurrection,
> to share his sufferings, in growing conformity with his death.

Nothing in the context has prepared us for this sudden reference to Christ's sufferings. Paul has simply been describing how the apparent advantages of his Jewish upbringing have turned out to be so much rubbish for the sake of gaining Christ. The sense would have been complete if he had broken off after 'the power of his resurrection': it was this, and the assurance of the righteousness acquired only through faith, which finally reduced everything that had gone before to 'loss'. But it may be that there is at least a hint in the previous sentences which should have prepared us for the mention of suffering. Paul has talked of himself as one who reckoned all his previous advantages as 'loss' compared with knowing Christ: it is he who has freely formed this judgement and made this decision. But into this repeated statement of his own deliberate reversal of values he inserts a passive verb (ἐζημιώθην): I *suffered* loss, I was penalized, suffered *hurt* and *damage*. This is not an altogether natural way of saying, 'I did in fact forfeit everything' (REB): in the passive the verb must mean that everything *was taken* from him, or that he was actually penalized.[15] If he had simply walked out of the synagogue never to return it is difficult to see how anything of this kind could have happened to him. But we know that this was not the case.[16] He received a severe – indeed the maximum – judicial flogging *five times*, as a result (we must assume) of being determined to enjoy access to the synagogue even though continuing to show contempt for certain 'observances of the law'. His own decision, that is to say, to renounce the superiority given to him by his parentage and education elicited a response from the synagogue which 'penalized' him very severely. It would be carrying speculation

---

[15] J. B. Lightfoot; *Philippians* (n. 15) 149 correctly translates, 'I suffered the confiscation, was mulcted, of ...'

[16] Cf. A. E. Harvey, 'Forty Strokes Save One' in A. E. Harvey, ed., *Alternative Approaches to New Testament Study*, 93–4.

too far to suggest that it was these floggings which caused his near-death experience (though they could well have done so, or at least made him more susceptible to other forms of illness or maltreatment). But if they were in his mind when he used the word 'penalized' it would be less surprising that his thought should have moved on to 'sharing Christ's sufferings'.

The important point to notice, at any rate, is that this sharing of Christ's sufferings is part of what Paul explicitly calls his 'gain' of Christ. It is, that is to say, something positive; and it is this which makes these words an unmistakable echo of 2 Corinthians 4. Suffering, by all normal standards, has negative value. It may have positive consequences, such as forming the character or even availing for others. But that it should be something of value in itself is a notion to which Paul had found his way (I have argued) only through the extremity he had recently endured. And this helps us to appreciate the force of the words that follow: 'in growing conformity with his death'. This expression is virtually equivalent to 2 Corinthians 4.10, 'carrying about the dying state (νέκρωσις) of Christ', and echoes the same experience. But by using the word 'conform' (συμμορφιζόμενοι) Paul relates it to a wider concept. Conform, transform: these 'form' (μορφ-) words[17] play a significant part in his analysis of Christian life and experience. Already in Galatians 4.9 he can speak of enabling Christ to be 'formed' in Christian converts; in Romans (8.29) he declares that they are predestined to be 'conformed' with the image of his son. This conformity involves transformation,[18] similar to, but also greatly superior to, that of Moses when exposed to the divine glory (2 Cor. 3.18); it implies 'renewal' of the mind (Rom. 12.2) – part of the 'inner man' that is 'renewed' even when the outer man is being destroyed (2 Cor. 4.16); but it depends also on total identification with Christ, not only in his present risen and glorious state, but in his suffering and death (Phil. 3.10). All of this becomes symbolically true for every Christian at the moment of baptism (Rom. 6.3–5), with immense ethical consequences: the power of sin and the tyranny of law are

---

[17] Well analysed by J. B. Lightfoot, *Epistle to the Philippians* (London, 1908) 127–33.

[18] The importance of 'transformation' in Paul's conversion experience has been persuasively argued in the light of Jewish mystical writings by Alan F. Segal, *Paul the Convert*, 58–71.

broken by this 'death'. But it becomes also an experienced reality in those sufferings to which a Christian is inevitably exposed and which are, not a barrier to belief in the saving power of the gospel, but a means to greater unity with Christ and a vehicle of that 'glory' which is to be revealed in greater splendour in the future (Rom. 8.18). The moment at which Paul experienced this reality and grasped its significance for the Christian life can be plausibly identified with his near-death experience recorded in 2 Corinthians 1.8.

'When we are afflicted, it is for your encouragement and salvation.' The explanation of this surprising phrase right at the beginning of 2 Corinthians (1.6) is in the account of the near-death experience which follows and in the working out of its implications later on. Equally surprising, at first sight, is the sudden appearance of 'you' in 4.12: 'death is at work in us, but life in you.' When studying that passage[19] we found it to be of a piece with Paul's conviction that his discovery of a positive value in suffering, and the consolation and reassurance that go with it, was by no means a private acquisition for himself or for any individual sufferer but extended its benefit widely to others. The same perception is brought to mind in the opening paragraph of the letter by a vivid image. A bowl or a glass, if it is less than full, may be simply filled up to capacity. But equally, the filling up may be so generous that it overflows and the surplus can be collected in other vessels or allowed to water the ground all about.[20] This is the image in 1.5: Christ's sufferings (or Christ-sufferings[21]) are awarded in such abundance that they *overflow* into the life of Paul, as a result of which the encouragement (παράκλησις) which derives from it *overflows* far beyond Paul's capacity to contain it and yields benefit to others. The same image reappears in the one passage that remains to be considered:

[19] See above p. 60.
[20] I owe this image to a personal note from C. H. Dodd:

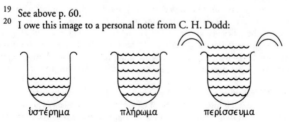

ὑστέρημα   πλήρωμα   περίσσευμα

[21] So Kümmel (*HNT* 196) and Martin 9–10. See n. 23.

Now I rejoice in my sufferings on your behalf and fill up in my own flesh that which remains unfilled[22] of Christ-sufferings[23] on behalf of his body, which is the church. (Col. 1.24 AT)

'That which remains unfilled' is the converse of an overflow: on the one hand a water jar stands half-empty, on the other hand it is being filled so generously that it overflows. The sufferings of the apostle, if they remain like a vessel not yet filled up, cannot overflow for the benefit of others in the church: they must be filled up in their turn[24] so that they may be 'on your behalf'; and it could well have been the memory of that exceptional near-death experience (or possibly a report of it)[25] which created this striking image for conveying its significance for the sufferer himself and for those who are 'consoled' or 'encouraged' by it.

This, of course, is not the angle from which the matter is usually approached. It is generally assumed that the explanation for the sometimes startling language Paul uses about suffering is to be sought not in biography but in theology. Paul's theological understanding of the relationship of believers with Christ, of their fellowship in his sufferings and their reconciliation through him to God, may have been in place long before; in which case his near-death experience, even if it was of a more traumatic character than any of his previous tribulations, will have been well prepared for by his long-standing

---

[22] Cf. Eduard Schweizer, *Der Brief an die Kolosser* (EKK) (Neukirchen-Vluyn, 1976) 85, who draws attention (n. 242) to the lack of solid evidence for the eschatological 'quota' of sufferings so dear to recent commentators.

[23] 'θλῖψις is nowhere in the N.T. demonstrably used of the actual sufferings of Jesus on the cross or in his ministry', C. F. D. Moule, *The Epistles to the Colossians and to Philemon* (Cambridge, 1957) 77.

[24] See J. B. Lightfoot, *Epistle to the Colossians* (London, 1904) 162–3, who adduces numerous parallels from classical Greek for the compound with ἀντι- meaning 'supplying *from an opposite quarter* to the deficiency' and translates 'I fill up on my part'. J. S. Pobee, *Persecution and Martyrdom in the Theology of Paul, JSNT* SS 6 (1985) 104 argues from other compounds with ἀντι- that the most likely meaning is 'in turn'. As Moule observes (78), Wettstein's simple comment may be correct: ἀντὶ ὑστερήματος succedit ἀνταναπλήρωμα.

[25] Schweizer (n. 22), 82 notes that this phrase goes beyond anything which can be found elsewhere in Paul, which is uncharacteristic of Colossians. If Colossians is not by Paul, I believe this verse must derive from something he was remembered to have written or said.

conviction of being constantly 'in Christ' and need not have had the crucial consequences I have been arguing for.

The classic example of this approach is that of Albert Schweitzer, who argued that for Paul, as for any Christian, membership of the Community of the Elect that was shortly to be revealed was guaranteed by 'a real co-experiencing of Christ's dying and rising again',[26] and that consequently Paul often 'speaks simply of dying where he might more logically speak simply of suffering'.[27] Suffering, according to this view, was an integral part of the Christian experience that began with baptism. The more acute it was, the easier it was to identify with the process of dying with Christ and the greater assurance it gave of the reality of 'being-in-Christ' and of being numbered among the Elect. Paul's near-death experience described in 2 Corinthians 1 is, from this perspective, no different from 'being buried with Christ' by being baptized into his death (Rom. 6.4), from 'dying to sin' (Rom. 6.2), or from being 'crucified with Christ' (Gal. 2.19). They are all phases of that 'dying and rising' which 'goes forward secretly but none the less really'[28] in every baptized Christian.

Even on its own terms Schweitzer's view would now need considerable revision. The fact that Paul used metaphors such as 'dying' in relation to sin or 'being crucified' in relation to the Law is hardly a sufficient explanation of the language with which he spoke of physical suffering and the threat of actual death: Paul nowhere calls these threatening experiences 'dying and rising with Christ'. But even if Schweitzer's theological construction has come to be generally rejected because of its over-emphasis on eschatology and its inappropriate category of 'Christ-mysticism', he has had many followers attempting the same task of giving a theological account of Paul's experience of suffering. This has been presented as a means of revealing Christ through the endurance of vicissitudes;[29] of allowing eschatological hope to transform present endurance;[30] or of assimilating into one world-

---

[26] A. Schweitzer, *The Mysticism of Paul the Apostle*, 13.

[27] Ib. 142.

[28] Ib. 110.

[29] E. Güttgemans, *Der Leidende Apostel und sein Herr* (FRLANT 90, Göttingen, 1966) following E. Käsemann, 'Die Legitimät des Apostels' *ZNW* 41 (1942) 33–71.

[30] W. Schrage, 'Leid, Kreuz und Eschaton' *Ev. Th.* 34 (1974) 141–175.

view the various strands of Jewish thinking on martyrdom and innocent suffering and of Christian reflection on Jesus' suffering, death and resurrection.[31] Studies of this kind have filled many volumes. Each gives due weight to at least part of the evidence. What all have in common is that they seek to integrate the various references which Paul makes to suffering and death into a theological system which Paul may be assumed to have affirmed throughout the period covered by his letters. If this is correct, clearly the near-death experience described in 2 Corinthians 1 will not have had the crucial significance I have been ascribing to it: Paul will have been spiritually prepared for such a crisis long before.

This approach, which may be called theological as opposed to biographical, has gone through a number of phases.[32] In the early years of this century it seemed as if the key to Paul's language about suffering and dying and being 'in Christ' could be found in the concepts of other ancient religions: it was these concepts which, suitably adapted, enabled him to come to terms with his experience as a Christian. With Schweitzer the emphasis shifted to Paul's eschatology and 'Christ-mysticism'. More recent studies have brought older Jewish categories of 'the righteous sufferer', of a martyr's vicarious suffering and of God's power to raise and reward the dead into a synthesis with Paul's Christian perceptions of the significance of Christ's death and of the believer's incorporation into his body. Structuralism has contributed the notion of the 'mimetic' function of suffering, offering a language in which to express the most elusive aspects of Christian experience.[33] This diversity of approach illustrates the difficulty of the task. Precisely how Paul held together his experiences of being 'buried with Christ', of having Christ 'living in him', of 'being renewed' – and many more – is a subject for continuing study and research.[34] But even if a consensus were to emerge it would be a complement rather than an alternative to my proposal. For it remains true that the texts upon which any

---

31 K. Kleinknecht, *Der Leidende Gerechtfertigte* (Tübingen, 1984).

32 Usefully summarized and documented by L. G. Bloomquist, *The Function of Suffering in Philippians* (*JSNTSS* 78, Sheffield, 1993) Part I.

33 D. Patte, *Paul's Faith, a Structuralist Introduction* (Philadelphia, 1983).

34 For a recent example, see the exhaustive study of 2 Cor. 10–13 by U. Heckel, *Kraft in Schwachheit* (WUNT 56, Tübingen 1993).

reconstruction of Paul's theology of suffering must be based occur in letters that were almost certainly written subsequent to the experience described in 2 Corinthians. Even if it was Paul's total understanding of the significance of Christ in the life of a Christian which enabled him to sustain the experience of being faced with the prospect of a sudden and premature death, it may still have been that experience itself which (as I have argued) was the catalyst and the endorsement of his thinking.

But how does all this compare with attitudes to suffering which we may believe to have been generally held by his contemporaries? We have already considered at some length the handling of such experiences by philosophers: their object and pride was to develop the resources that would enable them to sustain hardships and vicissitudes and maintain a philosophical detachment under every form of physical and mental tribulation. We saw that Paul was on occasion ready to allow his own adversities to be seen in a similar light, but that he ascribed his survival of them to a much more significant power than that of philosophy, and regarded them in any case as something he would refer to only in a moment of 'foolishness'. The really serious matter of suffering endured in solidarity with Christ was a world away from even the most Herculean endurance-feats of the philosophers.

But was there any comparable approach to suffering that he could have learnt from his Jewish contemporaries? It has to be said at once that by far the best attested and widely accepted view among Jewish people was that suffering was a consequence of sin.[35] The arguments of Job's comforters continued to carry the day for many centuries.[36] God is a God of justice: it seemed inconceivable that he would permit human beings to suffer in a manner that could not be somehow 'justified' by offences which, wittingly or unwittingly, had been committed and deserved punishment in this way. Paul himself evidently shared this view at times. The Jewish persecutors of the

---

[35] Cf. above, p. 24 n. 58. Also S. Schechter, *Studies in Judaism* (1896 repr. 1945) 214–26.
[36] Cf. the often quoted saying of R. Ammi, 'There is no death without sin, there is no suffering without sin', and Maimonides' endorsement of it, quoted by J. Bowker, *Problems of Suffering in the Religions of the World* (Cambridge, 1970) 32 n. 4.

church,[37] and the Gentile world in general (because of its immorality[38]), could expect to suffer by reason of their sin; and even Christians, if for instance they received the bread and the cup of the Lord unworthily, could expect to fall sick or even die.[39] Human beings clearly *are* responsible for much of the suffering endured by themselves or others. That the rabbis continued to regard sin as the prime cause of suffering is a measure of the seriousness with which they took the moral responsibility both of the nation and of the individual, even if it caused them to evade the anguished questioning of those whose suffering is clearly undeserved: it was an explanation that was to be found totally wanting in the face of the Shoah.[40]

But even in Paul's time other ways were being found of accounting for the apparently unjust and irrational distribution of suffering in the world. Suffering may be imposed on human beings for their good. It is a means by which God may test his children and form their character, either as individuals –

> My son, do not spurn the Lord's correction
> or recoil from his reproof:
> for those whom the Lord loves he reproves,
> and he punishes the son who is dear to him. (Prov. 3.11–12)

or as a nation –

> God never withdraws his mercy from us; although he may discipline his people by disaster, he does not desert them. (2 Macc. 6.16)

As a result, it was possible for the pious positively to welcome suffering. The famous story of Rabbi Aqiba laughing out loud when he found that he could say the *shema* even under torture by the Romans[41] is

---

[37] 1 Thess. 2.15–16.
[38] Rom. 2.18–32.
[39] 1 Cor. 11.30.
[40] N. de Lange, *Judaism* (Oxford, 1986) 122–124; C. Eimer in T. Bayfield and M. Braybrooke eds, *Dialogue with a Difference* (London, 1992) 97–101. It is not suggested for a moment that the traditional approach to suffering in Christianity or any religion has been adequate in the face of the Shoah.
[41] j. Ber. 9.7.

matched by a number of rabbinic sayings[42] to the effect that suffering was one of the gifts of God to his people, and Aqiba himself is reported to have said that 'sufferings are much to be loved'.[43] On this view, suffering is by no means always to be thought of as a punishment for sin; it may be a divinely appointed means of testing and disciplining the character – a view that Paul himself (like other New Testament writers[44]) endorsed on occasion, though its development into a positive welcome for suffering is attributed to rabbis who lived nearly a century after his time.

Yet this explanation, even if it ultimately enabled holy men to regard suffering as in some sense a blessing bestowed upon them by God, did not alter the fact that what had to be explained was an experience that is fundamentally evil, a kind of surd, something which ought not to occur in the life of a righteous individual and requires special explanation when it does so. It is true that a somewhat more positive approach had emerged from reflection on events in the Maccabean period.[45] Suffering came to be seen as part of the destiny of the people of God. It was a noble act, and one that might be required of a man by God, to endure suffering and death rather than be forced to transgress the commands of the divine law. Such suffering, indeed, might take on a vicarious significance such as was hinted at in Second Isaiah: it could be endured by the righteous as a means of atoning for the sins of their nation. Moreover, once belief in life after death had established itself, the problem of reconciling even the martyr's death with the justice of God began to receive an easy and confident solution. Those who had suffered in the cause of right would be amply rewarded hereafter.

Once again, it is possible to find in Paul instances of an approach to suffering along these lines. In 1 Corinthians 15 one of his arguments for the absolute necessity of faith in the resurrection is that it makes it possible to find a justification for the sufferings of the present (15.32):

---

[42] E.g. Ex. R. 30.13 (R. Aha).

[43] The extent to which R. Aqiba went beyond a received rabbinic view of suffering is somewhat controversial: see E. P. Sanders, 'R. Aqiba's View of Suffering' *JQR* 73 (1972–3) 332–51.

[44] See above, n. 12 and cf. Heb. 12.5–11.

[45] 4 Macc. 6.29; cf. W. H. C. Frend, *Martyrdom and Persecution in the Early Church* (Oxford, 1965) 55–8.

what has to be endured now (as Jesus seems repeatedly to have said) will be more than compensated for in the life to come. The same conviction is still evident when, in Romans, he speaks of present sufferings being unworthy to be compared with the glory that is to be revealed hereafter (8.18), and of our hope being attached to that which 'is not seen' (8.24). This language is similar to that which we have been studying in 2 Corinthians:

> Our troubles are slight and short-lived, and their outcome is an eternal glory which far outweighs them, provided our eyes are fixed, not on the things that are seen, but on the things that are unseen. (4.17–18)

Some have argued from this[46], and from the reference to judgement in 5.10, that this whole passage must be understood eschatologically: it is only in the light of what happens after death that the brute fact of suffering can be given any positive significance. Certainly Paul is writing as a man convinced of the reality of a future existence and of the rewards (as well as the awesome moment of judgement) that will belong to it. But this conviction by no means excludes a perception of the value of suffering here and now as a means of drawing closer to Christ. Hints of an eschatological solution to the problem of suffering do not invalidate the existential discovery which, I have argued, causes Paul to speak of the 'renewal of the inner man' here and now.

The same is true of the positive value which some Jewish thinkers were ascribing to the death of a martyr.[47] Paul evidently found comprehensible the notion of dying 'on behalf of a good man' (Rom. 5.7), and the language of sacrifice itself, which he can use of his own destiny as well as that of Christ (Phil. 2.17), shows that he was perfectly familiar with the idea of suffering being, in some sense, 'for others'. Yet none of this offers a sufficient precedent or parallel to the understanding of suffering which we find in 2 Corinthians. There, the suffering of the apostle (which is also shared by other Christians) is evidently endured in a spirit and with a reward which is quite new.

---

[46] For references, see above, ch. 3 nn. 23, 25, 26 and J. Lambrecht, 'The *Nekrōsis* of Jesus', in A. Vanhoye, ed. *L'Apôtre Paul* (BEThL, Louvain, 1986) 120–143.

[47] See above, p. 30 n. 64.

Now – as it seems for the first time, certainly in Paul and possibly in the history of religious thought[48] – suffering is not regarded as evil in itself, as something irrational or challenging to faith. Nor is it deliberately sought for or masochistically indulged in. There are no grounds for thinking that Paul would have commended severe physical mortification for its own sake: at most he subjected his body to a regime of self-discipline such as is necessary to equip anyone who lets every thought be taken prisoner for Christ (1 Cor. 9.27; 2 Cor. 10.5). But his experience of suffering bringing the sufferer closer to Christ, causing an inward renewal and spilling over into benefits for others, caused him to write of it as something of positive value in itself; and this, it seems, is without precedent in any Jewish or pagan sources known to us, and is hard to parallel in the revered writings of any other major religion. It is also the key, as I have tried to show in detail throughout this book, to the tense, personal, defensive but ultimately confident and generous argumentation of many parts of 2 Corinthians.

---

[48] I am not competent to make this more than a suggestion. But neither H. H. Rowley in his monograph, *Submission in Suffering: a comparative study of eastern thought* (Cardiff, 1942) nor J. Bowker, *Problems of Suffering* (above n. 36) offers anything comparable.

Bibliography

Ahern, B. M. 'The fellowship of his sufferings (Phil. 3.10)', *CBQ* 22 (1960) 1–32.

Allo, E.-B. *Saint Paul. Seconde Epître aux Corinthiens*, Etudes Bibliques (Paris, 1937).

Bailey, J. L. and Vander Broek, L. *Literary Forms in the New Testament* (London and Louisville USA, 1992).

Barré, M. L. 'To marry or to burn: πυροῦσθαι in 1 Cor. 7.9', *CBQ* 36 (1974) 193–202.

'Paul as "Eschatologic Person": A New Look at 2 Cor. 11:29', *CBQ* 37 (1975) 500–26.

'Qumran and the "Weakness" of Paul', *CBQ* 42 (1980) 216–27.

Barrett, C. K. *The Second Epistle to the Corinthians*, Black's New Testament Commentaries (London, 1973).

Barth, Karl *The Epistle to the Romans* (E.T. Oxford, 1933).

Beker, J. C. *Paul the Apostle. The Triumph of God in Life and Thought* (Philadelphia, 1980).

Belleville, Linda E. *Reflections of Glory*, *JSNTSS* 52 (Sheffield, 1991).

'Tradition or Creation? Paul's Use of the Exodus 34 Tradition in 2 Corinthians 3.7–18', in Craig A. Evans and James A. Sanders, eds., *Paul and the Scriptures of Israel*, *JSNTSS* 83 (Sheffield, 1993).

Berger, Klaus 'Almosen für Israel', *NTS* 23 (1977) 180–204.

Betz, H. D. 'Eine Christus-Apologie bei Paulus (2 Kor. 12.7–10)', *ZThK* 66 (1969) 288–303.

Der Apostel Paulus und die Sokratische Tradition, BHT 45 (Tübingen, 1972).

'2 Cor. 6.14–7.1: An Anti-Pauline Fragment?', *JBL* 92 (1973) 88–108.

2 Corinthians 8 and 9: A Commentary on Two Administrative Letters of the Apostle Paul, Hermeneia (Philadelphia, 1985).

Bloomquist, L. G. *The Function of Suffering in Philippians*, *JSNTSS* 78 (Sheffield, 1993).

Bowker, J. *Problems of Suffering in the Religions of the World* (Cambridge, 1970).

Bruce, F. F. *Paul, Apostle of the Free Spirit* (Exeter, 1977).

Bultmann, R. *Der Zweite Brief an die Korinther,* KEK (Göttingen, 1976).

Burton, E. de W. *A Critical and Exegetical Commentary on the Epistle to the Galatians,* ICC (Edinburgh, 1921).

Clavier, H. 'La Santé de l'Apôtre Paul', *Studia Paulina* (FS de Zwaan, Haarlem, 1953).

Collange, J.-F. *L'Epître de St Paul aux Philippiens* (Neuchâtel, 1973). *Enigmes de la deuxième épître de Paul aux Corinthiens* (Cambridge, 1972).

Collins, J. *Diakonia* (New York, 1991).

Cummins, S. A. see Goddard, A. J.

de Lange, N. *Judaism* (Oxford, 1986).

Delling, G. art. ἐπιτελέω, *TDNT* 8.62–3.

Derrett, J. Duncan M., '"ναί" (2 Cor. 1.19–20)', Filologia Neotestamentaria (Cordoba) 8 (1991), 205–9.

Dibelius, M. and Kümmel, W. *Paulus* (Berlin, 1956).

Dodd, C. H. *New Testament Studies* (Manchester, 1953).

Dunn, J. D. G. *Jesus and the Spirit* (London, 1975).

Edelstein, E. C. L. *Asclepius* (Baltimore, 1945).

Eimer, C. 'Suffering: A Point of Meeting' in T. Bayfield and M. Braybrooke, eds., *Dialogue with a Difference* (London, 1992).

Falk, Z. W. *Introduction to Jewish Law of the Second Commonwealth* (Leiden) I (1972), II (1978).

Fitzgerald, J. T. *Cracks in an Earthen Vessel: An Examination of the Catalogues of Hardships in the Corinthian Epistles,* SBLDS 99 (Atlanta, GA, 1988).

Forbes, C. 'Comparison, Self-praise and Irony: Paul's Boasting and the Conventions of Hellenistic Rhetoric', *NTS* 32 (1986) 1–30.

Ford, D. F. see Young, F.

Frend, W. H. C. *Martyrdom and Persecution in the Early Church* (Oxford, 1965).

Furnish, V. P. *II Corinthians*, Anchor Bible (Garden City, NY, 1984).

Georgi, D. *Die Gegner des Paulus im 2 Korintherbrief* (1964), E.T. *The Opponents of Paul in Second Corinthians*, SNTW (Edinburgh, 1987).

Goddard, A. J. and Cummins, S. A. 'Ill or ill-treated? Conflict and persecution as the context of Paul's original ministry in Galatia (Galatians 4.12–20)', *JSNT* 52 (1993) 93–126.

Godet, F. *La seconde épître aux Corinthiens* (Neuchâtel, 1914).

Güttgemans, E. *Der Leidende Apostel und sein Herr*, FRLANT 90 (Göttingen, 1966).

Hafemann, Scott J. *Suffering and Ministry in the Spirit* (USA: Grand Rapids, 1990).

Harvey, A. E. 'The Opposition to Paul', SE4 (1968) 319–332.

   Companion to the New Testament (Oxford and Cambridge, 1970).

   Jesus on Trial (London, 1976).

   Jesus and the Constraints of History (London, 1982).

   'The Workman is Worthy of his Hire', *NovT* 24 (1982) 209–221.

   'Forty Strokes Save One' in A. E. Harvey, ed., *Alternative Approaches to New Testament Study* (London, 1985) 79–96.

   'Christ as Agent', in L. D. Hurst and N. T. Wright, eds., *The Glory of Christ in the New Testament*, FS G. B. Caird (Oxford, 1987).

   Strenuous Commands: The Ethic of Jesus (London, 1990).

Heckel, U. 'Der Dorn im Fleisch, Die Krankheit des Paulus in 2 Kor. 12.7 and Gal. 4, 13f.', *ZNW* 84 (1993) 65–92.

   Kraft in Schwachheit, WUNT 56 (Tübingen, 1993).

Hengel, M. *The Pre-Christian Paul* (E.T. London and Philadelphia, 1991).

Héring, J. *La seconde Épître de Saint Paul aux Corinthiens* (Neuchâtel–Paris, 1958).

Hettlinger, R. F. '2 Corinthians 5.1–10', *SJT* 10 (1957) 179–94.

Hock, R. F. *The Social Context of Paul's Ministry* (USA: Fortress Press, 1980).

Hodgson, R. 'Paul the Apostle and First Century Tribulation Lists', *ZNW* 74 (1983) 59–80.

Hooker, Morna D. 'Interchange in Christ', *JTS* 22 (1971) 349–61.
'Interchange and Suffering', in W. Horbury and B. McNeil, eds.,
Suffering and Martyrdom in the New Testament (Cambridge, 1981)
71–83.

Hughes, F. W. 'The Rhetoric of Reconciliation: 2 Cor. 1.1–2.13 and
7.5–8.24', in D. F. Watson, ed., *Persuasive Artistry, JSNTSS* 50
(Sheffield, 1991).

Hughes, P. E. *Paul's Second Epistle to the Corinthians* (London, 1962).

Jewett, R. *Paul's Anthropological Terms* (Leiden, 1971).

Judge, E. A. 'The Conflict of Educational Aims in NT Thought',
Journal of Christian Education 9 (1966) 32–45.

Käsemann, E. 'Die Legitimät des Apostels', *ZNW* 41 (1942)
33–71.

Kent, H. A. 'The Glory of Christian Ministry. An analysis of 2 Cor.
2.14–4.18', *Grace Theological Journal* 2 (1981) 171–89.

Kleinknecht, K. *Der Leidende Gerechtfertigte* (Tübingen, 1984).

Kleinman, A. *Patients and healers in the context of culture* (University
of California Press, 1980).

Knox, J. *Chapters in a Life of Paul* (London, 1954).

Knox, W. L. *Paul* (London, 1932).

Lagrange, M.-J. *Saint Paul, Epître aux Galates* (Etudes Bibliques, Paris,
1942).

Lambrecht, J. 'The *Nekrosis* of Jesus' in A. Vanhoye, ed., *L'Apôtre Paul*
BEThL (Louvain, 1986).

Lang, F. G. *2. Korinther 5.1–10 in der Neueren Forschung*, BGBE 16
(Tübingen, 1973).

Lietzmann, H. *An die Römer HNT* 8³ (Tübingen, 1928).
An die Korinther I/II *HNT* 9⁴, with supplement by W. G. Kümmel
(Tübingen, 1949).

Lightfoot, J. B. *St Paul's Epistles to the Colossians and to Philemon*,
New Edition (London, 1879).
St Paul's Epistle to the Philippians, Fourth Edition (London, 1885).
St Paul's Epistle to the Galatians, Tenth Edition (London, 1890).

Litfin, D. *St Paul's Theology of Proclamation, SNTSMS* 79 (Cambridge, 1994).

Lohmeyer, E. *Die Briefe an die Philipper, Kolosser und an Philemon* KEK⁹ (Göttingen, 1953).

Lowther Clarke, W. K., ed., *Liturgy and Worship* (London, 1932).

Lüdemann, G. *Paul, Apostle to the Gentiles: Studies in Chronology* (London, 1984).

Lyons, G. *Pauline Autobiography: Toward a new Understanding*, SBLDS 73 (Atlanta, GA, 1985).

Malherbe, A. J. *Paul and the Popular Philosophers* (Minneapolis, 1989).

Manson, T. W. '2 Cor. 2.14–17: Suggestions towards an exegesis', *Studia Paulina*, FS de Zwaan (Haarlem, 1953) 155–62.

Martin, R. P. *2 Corinthians*, Word Biblical Commentary (Waco, TX, 1986).

Mommsen, T. *Römisches Strafrecht* (Leipzig, 1899).

Moore, G. F. *Judaism* (Harvard, 1927).

Moule, C. F. D. *The Epistles to the Colossians and to Philemon* (Cambridge, 1957).

'St Paul and Dualism: the Pauline Conception of Resurrection', *NTS* 12 (1965–6) 106–23.

Mullins, T.Y. 'Paul's Thorn in the Flesh', *JBL* 76 (1957) 299–303.

Newman, C. C. *Paul's Glory-Christology, NovT Supp.* 69 (Leiden, 1992).

Neyrey, J. *Paul, in Other Words* (Louisville, 1990).

Olson, S. N. 'Pauline Expressions of Confidence in his Addressees', *CBQ* 47 (1985) 282–95.

Oostendorp, D. W. *Another Jesus: A Gospel of Jewish-Christian Superiority in II Corinthians* (Kampen, 1967).

Patte, D. *Paul's Faith, a Structuralist Introduction* (USA: Fortress Press, 1983).

Plummer, A. *A Critical and Exegetical Commentary on the Second Epistle of St Paul to the Corinthians*, ICC (Edinburgh, 1915).

Pobee, J. S. *Persecution and Martyrdom in the Theology of Paul, JSNTSS* 6 (Sheffield, 1985).

Robinson, J. A. T. *Wrestling with Romans* (London, 1979).

Rowley, H. H. *Submission in Suffering: a comparative study of eastern thought* (Cardiff, 1942).

Sanders, E. P. 'R. Aqiba's View of Suffering', *JQR* 73 (1972–3) 332–51.
Paul and Palestinian Judaism (London, 1977).

Sargant, W. *Battle for the Mind* (London, 1957).

Schechter, S. *Studies in Judaism* (Philadelphia, 1896 repr. 1945).

Schlier, H. *Der Brief an die Galater*, KEK (Göttingen, 1949).
art. ἐκπτύω, *TWNT* 2.446–7 (1964).

Schmithals, W. *Die Gnosis in Korinth* (1956; ²1965) E.T. *Gnosticism in Corinth* (New York and Nashville, 1971).

Schmitz, O. art. παρακαλέω *and* παράκλησις, *TDNT* 5, 790–798.

Schrage, W. 'Leid, Kreuz und Eschaton', *EvTh* 34 (1974) 141–75.

Schweitzer, A. *The Mysticism of Paul the Apostle* (E.T. London, 1931).

Schweizer, E. *Der Brief an die Kolosser*, EKK (Neukirchen-Vluyn, 1976).

Seeley, D. *The Noble Death, JSNTSS* 28 (Sheffield 1990).

Segal, A. F. *Paul the Convert: the Apostolate and Apostasy of Saul the Pharisee* (Yale, 1990).

Seybold, K. *Das Gebet des Kranken im Alten Testament* (BWANT 99, Stuttgart etc., 1973).

Seybold, K. and Mueller, U. *Sickness and Healing* (USA: Abingdon Press, 1978–81).

Sherwin-White, A. N. *Roman Society and Roman Law in the New Testament* (Oxford, 1963).

Stendahl, K. *Paul among Jews and Gentiles* (London, 1977).

Theissen, G. *The Miracle Stories of the Early Christian Tradition* (E.T. SNTW Edinburgh, 1983).

Thrall, M. E. *A Critical and Exegetical Commentary on the Second Epistle to the Corinthians*, vol. I, ICC (Edinburgh, 1994).

van der Horst, P. *The Sentences of Pseudo-Phocylides* (Leiden, 1978).

van Unnik, W. C. '"With Unveiled Face", an Exegesis of 2 Corinthians
iii 12–18' *NovT* 6 (1963) 153–69.
'The Semitic Background of παρρησία in the New Testament',
Sparsa Collecta 2, *NovT Supp.* 30 (1980) 290–306.

Watson, F. '2 Cor. 10–13 and Paul's Painful Visit to the Corinthians'
JTS 35 (1984) 324–46.
Weiser, A. *The Psalms* (E.T. London, 1962).
Wettstein, J. J. *Novum Testamentum Graecum* (Amsterdam, 1751–2).
Windisch, H. *Der Zweite Korintherbrief KEK*⁹ (Göttingen, 1924).
Wiseman, J. art. 'Corinth' *ANRW* II 7.1 (1979).

Young, Frances and Ford, D. F. *Meaning and Truth in 2 Corinthians*
(London, 1987).

Index of References

Old Testament

Genesis

	3	97f.
	8.21	45

Exodus

	16.18	85
	25.40	66
	33.11	52
	34.28	48
	34.29	48
	34.34	50

Leviticus

	6.28	55

Numbers

	15.27–31	84
	33.55	10

Deuteronomy

	19.15	108

Esther

	16.9 Vg	39

Psalms

	5.12 LXX	34
	22.12–13	12
	22.14–15	12
	30.13 LXX	57
	31.11 LXX	34
	37.5 LXX	18
	38	18
	38.10–11	22
	38.15	26
	41.11–12	26
	69.8–14	24f.
	88.17 LXX	33
	114.3–8 LXX	18
	114.4 LXX	32
	115.1 LXX	18
	116	18, 61
	116.1	32
	116.4–7	32
	116.18	32
	118.17–18	25, 74
	118.32 LXX	75

Proverbs

	3.4 LXX	86
	3.11–12	118, 126
	11.24	90
	17.6	33
	22.8 LXX	90

Ecclesiastes

	7.29	62

Isaiah

	49.8	74
	49.13	78
	54.5–6	97
	62.5	97

Jeremiah

	9.22–3 LXX	97
	9.23 LXX	33
	31.31–34	42
	31.33	47

Ezekiel

	1.28	52
	16.8	97

28.24 LXX   10

Hosea
2.19–20   97

Apocrypha

Tobit
3.17 Vg   39

Wisdom of Solomon
5.1   77
9.15   66

2 Maccabees
6.16   126
6.28   30
6.31   30

4 Maccabees
6.29   127
7.8   30

New Testament

Matthew
18.16   108

Mark
14.58   67

Luke
4.19ff.   74

John
5.31   108
8.14ff.   108
8.17   108

Acts
11   116

14.19   102
15   116
16.22   101
16.23   74
17   87
18.18   87
20.1–13   116

Romans
2.18–32   126
5.7   128
6.1–11   117
6.2   123
6.3   117
6.3–5   120
6.4   117, 123
6.5   117
6.6   117
6.12ff.   70
7   6, 63
7.22f.   62, 63
8.1–13   94
8.3–4   62
8.13–14   70
8.17   117
8.18   118, 121, 128
8.24   128
8.29   120
12.2   120
12.9   74
12.17   86
16.1   87

1 Corinthians
2   98
2.4   35, 95
3.16   67
4.14   105
4.15   105
9.2   98
9.27   129
10.11   8

10.13	118	3.6	48
11.29–30	27	3.7	50
11.30	126	3.11	50
11.32	118	3.12	50, 51
15.23	27	3.13	50, 58
15.30–31	118	3.18	52, 72, 120
15.32	112, 127	4.1	52
15.51–52	27	4.1–4	71
		4.2	54, 93
2 Corinthians		4.3–4	54
1.1	87	4.6	54
1.3	8, 9, 16	4.7	55
1.4	17	4.8ff.	56, 74
1.5–6	121	4.10	58, 72, 94, 120
1.8	2, 8, 9, 18, 57,	4.11	68, 94
	64, 81, 107, 121	4.12	60, 77, 121
1.8–10	112	4.14	61
1.9	19	4.15	60
1.10	53	4.16	61, 62f., 120
1.10–11	32	4.17	64
1.12	34, 36, 72	4.17–18	128
1.13	36	4.17–5.5	61
1.15–22	38	4.18	64
1.15	36, 38	5.1–4	65
1.17	36, 38, 94	5.5	69
1.21–22	42	5.6	69
1.23	42	5.9	69, 71
1.24	43	5.10	68, 70, 98, 128
2.1	38	5.11	98
2.4	44, 78, 95	5.12	71, 93
2.5	43, 44	5.13	71
2.6	44	5.16	72
2.7	44	5.17	72
2.8	44	6.1	73
2.9	44	6.2	74
2.10	44	6.4–10	74
2.12–13	78	6.9	25, 75, 118
2.12–15	48	6.14–7.1	75f., 92
2.14	45	7	44
2.16	46, 48	7.4	77
3	64, 117	7.5–12	43
3.1	46, 93	7.6	78

7.16	78
8.1	81
8.1–5	87
8.3–5	82
8.6	84
8.9	83
8.10–11	88
8.17	85
8.18–19	106
8.20	94
9	87f.
9.2	88
9.6	90
9.7	90
9.8–10	90
10–13	92f.
10.1	93, 95
10.2	94
10.3	99
10.4	102
10.4–5	95f.
10.5	129
10.8	33, 96
10.9–11	96
10.10	95
10.12–13	97
10.12–16	97
10.14	96
10.16	97
11	15, 33
11.1	97
11.4	98
11.6	36, 95, 98
11.7	99
11.10	99
11.11	99
11.16	99
11.18	99
11.21	100
11.22–23	101
11.23	74, 101
11.25–26	118

12	33
12.2	103f.
12.6–7	103
12.7	9, 10
12.10	104
12.12	105
12.13	98, 105
12.17–18	75
12.18	106
12.19	107
12.21	107
13.1	108
13.3	109
13.5	110
13.5–10	110
13.7	110

Galatians

1	14
2.15–21	116
2.19	58, 116, 117, 123
3.13	116
3.27	67
4.9	120
4.12–15	22
4.13	95
4.13–15	10
4.19	105, 110
5.19–21	94
5.22–25	70
5.25	74
6.17	116

Ephesians

3.10	67

Philippians

1.21ff.	19
1.29	118
2.17	128
2.26	23
2.30	23

3.6	6	
3.8	119	
3.10	119f.	
4.5	27	
4.10–19	81	
4.14–19	40	

Colossians
1.24	31, 122	
3.9–10	67	

1 Thessalonians
1.6	118	
2.9	9	
2.15–16	126	
2.16	7	
4.15–17	26	
4.16	27	

2 Thessalonians
3.8	9	
3.9	98	

1 Timothy
1.13	4	
5.19	108	

Titus
3.5	63	

Philemon
10	105	

Hebrews
9.11	67	
12.5–11	127	

1 Peter
1.8	69	

2 Peter
3.16	41	

Early Jewish Writings

Ascension of Isaiah   103

Psalms of Solomon
10.1–3	24	

Dead Sea Scrolls
1 QS 4.23	62	

Mishnah
Berakoth	3.5	65
Makkoth	3.14	20

Jerusalem Talmud
Berakoth	9.7	126

Babylonian Talmud
Makkoth	5b	109

Midrashim
Midrash ha-gadol
Ex. 34.33	49	

Exodus Rabbah
33.1	49	
47.5	49	

Leviticus Rabbah
30.6	108	

Pesiqta Rabbati
10.6	49	

Greek and Latin Authors

Aristotle
Mirabilia	845a	45
Rhetorica	1.13	84
	3.15.1	107

Dio Chrysostom
  Orationes   42.5   36
                  77.1–2   36

Epictetus
  Dissertationes
              4.7.13–15   56
              4.8.27–29   33

Euripedes
  *Andromache*164–5   95
  Orestes   307–8   77

Gregory Nazianzenus
  Epistulae   152   58

Hermas
  Visions   3.8.9   63

Horace
  Satirae   2.3.35   10

Ignatius
  Ephesians   20.2   45
  Trallians   6.2   45

Jerome
  Epistulae 121.10.4   105

John Chrysostom
  *ad 2 Cor.*1.17   37
  *ad 2 Cor.*3.18   52
  *ad 2 Cor.*6.1   72
  homilia 3 in 1 Tim.   4

Marcus Aurelius Antoninus
              8.48   56

Origen
  Commentarii in Rom.,
    praefatio   3

Philo
  De Decalogo
              112–120   105
  De Somniis 1.158   73
                2.228   49
  De Vita Contemplativa
              75   36
  Legum Allegoriae
              3.101   52
              3.102   66
  Quod Deus Immutabilis sit
              87   73
  Quis Rerum Divinarum Heres
              141–206   85
              191   85
  Vita Mosis   2.70   49
                   2.245   105

Philostratus
  *Vita Apollonii*1.13   46

Plato
  Phaedrus   277e   35
  Protagoras   313d   46
  Republic   406 c–e   21
                589a   62
  Symposium 216 d–e   62

Plutarch
  De Alexandri magna fortuna
              327c   100
  De laude ipsius   15
  Galba 17   106

Pseudo-Philo
  Liber Antiquitatum Biblicarum
              12.1   49

Pseudo-Phokylides
              51–2   84

Quintilian
   Institutiones Oratoriae
       2.15.3   71

Seneca
   Epistulae   59.8   56
              82.14 56
              95.57 84
   De Providentia 5.4   106

Simonides 542 PMG   22

Tertullian
   De Pudicitia
       13.15–16   11

Theophrastus
   Characteres 22.3   89

Index of Modern Authors

Ahern, B.M., 2
Allo, E.-B., 71

Bailey, J.L., 3
Barré, M.L., 102, 104
Barrett, C.K., 16, 55, 71, 86
Barth, Karl, 79
Beker, J.C., 3
Belleville, Linda E., 49, 52
Berger, K., 91
Betz, H.D., 75, 80, 81, 82, 83, 84, 85, 86, 89, 90, 91, 104, 115
Bloomquist, L.G., 22, 124
Bower, J., 125, 129
Bruce, F.F., 2, 116
Bultmann, R., 77
Burton, E. de W., 116

Calvin, J., 23
Clavier, H., 10
Collange, J.-F., 19, 50
Collins, J., 83, 101
Cummins, S.A., 22

de Lange, N., 126
Delling, G., 83
Derrett, J. Duncan M., 40, 43
Dibelius, M., 10
Dodd, C.H., 7,8,121

Edelstein, E.C.L., 21
Eimer, C., 126

Falk, Z.W., 109
Fitzgerald, J.T., 15, 16, 29, 56, 58, 74, 75

Forbes, C., 15, 83
Ford, D.F., 93
Frend, W.H.C., 127

Gallas, S., 101
Georgi, D., 92
Goddard, A.J., 22
Godet, F., 50
Güttgemans, E., 123

Hafemann, Scott J., 45, 46
Harvey, A.E., 21, 35, 41, 60, 62, 73, 77, 89, 99, 101, 108, 109, 116, 119
Heckel, U., 10, 33, 63, 124
Hengel, M., 2
Héring, J., 49
Hettlinger, R.F., 64
Hock, R.F., 21, 74, 99
Hodgson, R., 100
Hooker, Morna D., 60, 118
Hughes, F.W., 16
Hughes, P.E., 81

Jewett, R., 63
Judge, E.A., 102

Käsemann, E., 123
Kent, H.A., 50
Kleinknecht, K., 124
Kleinman, A., 11
Knox, J., 92
Knox, W.L., 5
Kümmel, W.G., 45, 50
Lagrange, M.-J., 10
Lambrecht, J., 128

Lang, F.G., 64
Lietzmann, H., 45, 46, 50, 93, 96, 98, 107
Lightfoot, J.B., 9-11, 22, 116, 119, 120, 122
Litfin, D., 14, 35
Lohmeyer, E., 23
Lowther Clarke, W.K., 59
Lüdemann, G., 92
Lyons, G., 14

Malherbe, A.J., 29, 30, 95
Manson, T.W., 45
Martin, R.P., 16, 18, 19, 65, 72, 75, 87
Mayser, E., 86
Mommsen, T., 101
Moore, G.F., 24
Moule, C.F. D., 67, 122
Mueller, U., 11, 104
Mullins, T.Y., 11

Newman, C.C., 51
Neyrey, J., 23

Olson, S.N., 78
Oostendorp, D.W., 92

Patte, D., 124
Plummer, A., 39, 97, 115
Pobee, J.S., 122

Robinson, J.A.T., 6

Rowley, H.H., 129

Sanders, E.P., 6, 127
Sargant, W., 5
Schechter, S., 125
Schmithals, W., 92
Schmitz, O., 16, 83
Schrage, W., 123
Schweitzer, A., 10, 123
Schweizer, E., 122
Seeley, D., 30
Segal, A.F., 52, 72, 103, 120
Seybold, K., 11, 13, 22, 104
Sherwin-White, A.N., 101
Stendahl, K., 5

Theissen, G., 21
Thrall, M.E., 46, 52, 53, 67, 72

Vander Broek, L., 3
van der Horst, P., 105, 116
van Unnik, W.C., 51

Watson, F., 115
Weiser, A., 13
Wettstein, J.J., 45, 122
Windisch, H., 9, 36, 43, 45, 48, 49, 50, 53, 62, 64, 66, 72, 86, 87, 89, 97-9, 101, 106, 107
Wiseman, J., 87

Young, Frances, 65, 93

General Index

Achaia   87f.
Acts, reliability of   2, 92n.
Aelius Aristides   12n.
Agency   73
Ammi, Rabbi   125n.
Anaphora   39
Aqiba, Rabbi   126f.
Authority   43f., 91, 96
Autobiography   13, 14, 117

Baptism   67, 117, 120
Betrothal   97
Biography   1, 4, 7, 112ff.
Boasting   15, 33, 99, 102, 103f.
Burden, Burdening   22

Chronology   7f.
Civil Service   81ff., 85
Collection   106
Commendation, letters of   47
Commission   85f., 106
'Comparison'   15, 83
Consolation   16f., 28, 118
Corinthian correspondence   114f.
Corinth   87f.
Cynics   15, 24, 29, 30,
                          56, 75, 96n.

Democracy   86
Demon-possession   23
Disease   11f.
Doxa   51ff.

Epaphroditus   23
Equality   85
Eyes, complaint of   10

Fickleness   37ff.
Flesh,   94, 99
    see Wisdom, fleshly
Foolishness   97, 105

Gamaliel   1
Generosity   82
Glory   47ff., 51ff.

Hercules   29, 30

Illness   11f.
    consequences of   21ff.
Intention   84

Jesus   58ff., 72, 116ff.
Judgement   70

Kabod   51

Legal procedure   107ff.
Letters
    of commendation   47
Lists
    see Tribulation lists
Luther, Martin   4

Maccabees   30n., 127
Macedonia   82f.
Martyrdom   128f.
Moral standards   70
Moses   47ff.
Musonius Rufus   56n.
Mysticism   71, 103f.

Nakedness   65n.

Nekrōsis   58f.
Negotiation   40
Nero   2
Notker Balbulus   59

Origen   3n.
Outward-inward   62f.
Overflow   121

Paraklēsis   16f., 77f., 93, 121
Paraclete   17
Paul
    attitude to Jews   7
    autobiography of   13
    biography of   1, 4, 7, 112ff.
    boasting   15, 33, 99, 102, 103f.
    conversion   2, 4ff.
    credibility   37
    death   2
    fickleness, alleged   37ff.
    financial support for   98f.,
                                  105f.
    future expectations   8, 26f.
    illness   11f.
    journeys   2
    mysticism   71, 103ff.
    near-death experience   9ff.,
            113f., 117f., 122, 124
    prayer   18
    theology   122ff.
    understanding of suffering   31,
                                  123ff.
    weakness   95
    as letter-writer   3
    as scripture   3
Philosophy   56f., 62, 66, 74,
                 96n., 100, 125
    and wisdom   34f.
Pottery   55f., 57
Poverty   82, 91
Pride   32ff.
Prodigal Son   73

Psalms   12, 18, 25, 32
Psychology, Freudian   5

Qumran   56

Reconciliation   72f.
Renewal   63, 120, 128
Resurrection   113
Rhetoric   14, 35f., 71n.,
                  83, 100, 107

Satan   99
Second coming   8, 26f.
Serpent   98n.
Servant, service   83, 101
Shoah   126
Solomon   90
Sophists   35
Spirit, of God   69
Stoics   15, 24, 56, 74, 96n.
Suffering,
    explanations of   28f., 125ff.
    understanding of   28, 31,
                              116, 118
    understanding (Jewish) of 125ff.
Super-apostles   98
Symptoms   12

Tarsus   1
Taxation   9, 40n.
Temple   66f.
Thorn in the flesh   10, 104
Titus   44, 78, 81, 85f., 106
Transformation   72, 120
Tribulation lists   15, 56ff.,
                           74f., 100ff.

Veil   49ff., 58

Wealth   82
Wisdom   34ff., 89f.
    fleshly   34